Five Steps Healing from Grief

Me after *You*

Surviving the
Loss of a Loved One

by GIGI VEASEY, LCSW, LISAC, CCBT

*This book
is dedicated to*

my dear friend

Monica Claros Hammond

who continues to

inspire me to live fully.

And to my father Jess Veasey

who inspired my education

and sense of adventure.

Table of Contents

SECTION TWO
The Five Written Expressions of Grief

S E C T I O N   T H R E E

*The Longer Journey
Toward Healing*

The first
step is always
the hardest.

TURN THE PAGE.

YOUR JOURNEY TO

HEALING BEGINS

ACKNOWLEDGMENTS

This is my first book. It has truly been a labor of love and passion. Several people in my life have helped fuel this passion and drive. I would like to acknowledge my Husband Larry, who was the first to say, "You need to write a book!" This book began with the loss of my friend Monica Claros Hammond. I don't know if I would have started writing if I hadn't lost her—thanks for that gift Monica. I want to thank my book coaches Gina Kilker and Natalie Kilker for their guidance and reassurance that I had something important to say and the talented Chellie Buzzeo for her beautiful artwork and book design. Thanks to Lisa Jane Vargas for connecting me with them.

With much gratitude I acknowledge 'My Peeps' Tom and Lou Mongan who I met by-chance and who have encouraged me as they saw the gravity of my message as well as volunteering to assist in editing this book. Much appreciation to my awesome office assistants Tanya Lombardi who sat with me and gave me feedback to make sure it all made sense to my audience, and Karen Mienerz who was a warm compassionate sounding board. Warm appreciation to Billy Ryan who saw the importance of my message and became my "number one" fan to get my intensive grief/loss workshops into the recovering community.

I want to acknowledge my best friend Kris Volcheck who has stood beside me in all my professional endeavors over the last 30 years. A big thanks to Renee' Siegel who helped me stay balanced and to Melissa Thornburg who had faith in my project and helped me connect with a publisher so I could get my message out to the world. I want to recognize my circle of supportive, "you got this" friends who continually encouraged me and showed enthusiasm for this project and faith in my message: Jennifer Hecker-DuVal, Colleen Kumia, Rick and Jolene Baney, Merilee Reynolds, Michael Warren, Ericka Irvin, Norma Dulin, Lucille Heaney, Kiera Lane, Vicki Miller, and Karen Shelton.

I would also like to give gratitude to Elizabeth Kubler-Ross for her ground-breaking work in the field of grief/loss and death/dying. I want to mention Beverly Ryan whose Hospice work and caring helped families communicate in healthy ways at the end of life. It takes a village to write a book.

Thank you all

FOREWORD

As both my professional colleague and personal friend, Gigi Veasey is a force to be reckoned with. As the Executive Director of a highly reputable treatment center, characterized by long-standing and proven recovery programs, I entrust the care of our patients to only the most respectable and proficient professionals and staff. In this discerning capacity, Gigi joined our recovery team three years ago, providing grief counseling to our patients through her intensive workshops. In the time facilitating her grief workshops, I've often been awestruck and amazed by Gigi's clinical excellence, boundless compassion, and contagious devotion to guiding her patients through life's most complex and difficult journey—grief. I've seen the force of her spirit in action, witnessing the indelible impacts of her care and expertise on countless patient's lives. Yet, her true impact shines well beyond our immediate understanding, and the work she does moves through us and heals us for the rest of our lives.

My relationship with Gigi Veasey has come packaged with several fascinating paradoxes, each revealing her ubiquitous influence. The first paradox came quickly when we were introduced by a mutual friend and colleague. Despite having never met Gigi before that moment, I somehow felt as if I'd known her my whole life. Behind her handshake and kind words of conversational prelude was an unmistakable depth of soul, spirit, and wisdom—a kind of timeless quality to her physical bearing, soothing voice, and healing energies. As you'll undoubtedly discover in your book journey with Gigi, I was met head-on by her drive and passion for sharing her healing techniques, unique perspectives, and wisdom on the gritty issues of grief and loss.

As I got to know Gigi, I learned about the steadfast and scrupulous honing of her expertise, the basis of her representation of hope and healing. I came to know about her 40-plus years of experience in assisting people through extremely difficult and trying times of loss, grief, and bereavement. And again, despite a background steeped in apparent emotional and spiritual heaviness and mournful experiences, when Gigi assists her patients, providing comfort, education, and guidance, she exhibits a wonderful lightness of being in her interactions that balances and contrasts against the trauma of loss. Her disarming smile, deeply caring heart, and keen gaze are constant reminders that in grief there can be hope, in guidance through intricate therapy concepts there can be occasional humor, and in the depths of incredible sorrow – healing.

In observing Gigi's workshops, I've witnessed a third paradox, one that may be familiar to anyone who has ever engaged in the processes of meditation and self-reflection. In this introspective process, it is often observed that the more one applies oneself to the difficult and often-arduous task of fully engaging with and facing one's grief, and the accompanying and subsequent onslaught of dizzying and clanging emotions, the more one is rewarded with a profound sense of relief, joy, and ability to 'keep on keeping on'. Gigi understands this paradox and, in her workshops as in this book, she serves as a gentle, yet masterful guide from the emotional depths to its heights.

I know that most people picking up this book likely feel that their personal circumstance and experience of loss is truly unique. You may think to yourself that no one else in the world can really understand what you're going through, know the anguish you're feeling, or feel the depth of loss as you've lost. And while true—we are all certainly unique—Gigi has an innate ability to help you feel connected to the rest of the human race, with all of us who have lost beyond measure. In this book she will allow you space to be singularly you, while nevertheless also providing you the tools to reconnect and re-engage with the people who love you and still need you to be uniquely you!

I predict, dear reader, that you will likely encounter the fifth, and final paradox of Gigi Veasey's work. And, in doing so, I encourage you to push through it, to face it head-on and with open arms, believing in the conviction of her methods and the healing in her process. In your sadness it is quite possible you might be tempted to NOT want to read this book; just picking it up off the table or nightstand may come perilously close to bringing up more sorrow and tears. But please turn the page. I guarantee that in confronting this paradox, you'll find every page to provide another step closer to healing and hope.

I treasure the day I was first introduced to Gigi and finally dear reader, it's your turn! Settle in, get comfortable, get to know Gigi as I have, and please allow her to guide you through the processes of discovering renewed meaning of life and emotional and spiritual peace. In these pages that follow, Gigi takes us from these five paradoxes to what she calls *The Five Written Expressions of Grief.*

They are powerful, they work, and they will help you. I promise!

David Anderson, Ph.D.
Licensed Psychologist
Executive Director,
The Meadows,
Wickenburg, AZ

The Birth of a Book:
Who am I and Why am I Writing About Grief?

By the time I was four years old, I knew I wanted to help people and by the ripe old age of five I knew my vehicle to that end would be Nursing. I was the kid who slapped bandages on my friends when they fell off their bikes. I had watched enough television by the age of nine that I would make statements like "move back, give him some air" and had mastered my favorite medical term... wait for it..."contusion." My "Baby Nancy Nurse" doll and I were on the scene. I followed this dream all the way through high school when I became a candy striper, donned the red and white striped smock and headed off to the local hospital to visit patients.

In college I majored in Nursing and made it through all but my practicum before I began to question my choice. I attended a Nursing Student Club meeting where a "real" Nurse came to talk to us about Nursing. I was so excited; I took in all she had to say, landing on an interpretation that wasn't living up to the image I had held since childhood. After all I had learned and the amount of knowledge required to be a Nurse, this description of the profession sounded as if that knowledge was not all necessary and I would not be able to apply a portion of it. I had seen myself drifting down the halls of hospitals caring for patients in a compassionate and calm manner while putting to use all the knowledge I had attained in school. I wanted to be part of a team and soak up additional wisdom in the Nursing and Medical fields. I was not interested in just handing out medications and starting IV's, I wanted more and my gut said I would not be happy with Nursing. This led to some confused days and weeks; I had been planning on being a Nurse for as long as I could remember. I was still clear I wanted to help people. I thought of going to medical school and also had thoughts about majoring in Pharmacy or Physical Therapy.

I was fascinated by Psychology, another avenue for helping people, and began taking some courses when I ran into a single paragraph in a reading assignment titled "Medical Social Work." I read it twice, I had no idea there was a career path where I could combine my desire and interest in the medical field with Psychology, and it felt magical, almost too good to be true. After reading this, I closed my book, walked to campus and searched for my professor. Luckily he was available and I told him, "This is me! How do I do this?" I shifted my major from Nursing to Sociology/Social Work, got the necessary Masters in Social Work, and started my 20-year career on that path. For me, it was like finding that pesky puzzle piece after trying to fit six other pieces into the spot, it just fit and my whole soul knew it intuitively.

My first job was as a Director of Social Services in a hospital at the time of the HIV/AIDS epidemic. There was so much loss and grief. The fear surrounding this disease was palpable. Patients, family and staff were feeling helpless as knowledge about contagion and treatment changed, sometimes on a weekly basis. I learned to be present and supportive for patients and families in those overwhelming times. I wanted to do something to change this fearful environment, so I began to work with the CDC and a local AIDS organization to develop a mandatory education program for all staff. This program would give staff the latest information and help answer some questions that caused fear. This program then became a part of new employee orientation.

I moved on to work at another hospital as part of the heart transplant team and candidate selection committee for transplant where I supported, educated, and advocated for patients and their families. I wore the pager (dating myself) proudly and waited for those magical calls when a heart match arrived and the team saved a life. My last full-time position was working in a neurological center in the Neuro Intensive Care Unit (NICU) with new traumatic brain injury and spinal cord injury patients.

I learned so much about the field of medicine over these years, the reality of trauma and how life can change in an instant. I had the opportunity and privilege to be present for hundreds of patients and families over the years as they struggled through the devastation of losing a loved one. I learned to live this life fully and to be present in each moment and with each person. There are no guarantees; none of us know how long we will be here. I focused on the quality of my life and looked deeper at how I wanted to live as well as what wishes I had for the end. I wanted to relieve my loved ones of the burden of guessing or making those final decisions on my behalf by putting a Living Will in place. These were gifts I received from my experiences.

After 20 years in hospitals as a Medical Social Worker, I started my private practice, focusing on what I knew best, grief and loss. The culmination of my hospital work, my private practice experience with grieving clients and my personal experiences of loss, led me to develop a therapeutic process called *The Five Written Expressions of Grief*™(5WE's). I was searching for a way to be more helpful, to encourage my patients and clients to express and release thoughts and feelings they were carrying. I considered where people may feel stuck and helpless and what might make a difference in the heaviness of their hearts. The 5WE's guide and ease loved ones going through the grief process. After using this method for over 25 years in individual counseling and grief/loss workshops, I have seen the pain of my client's ease, or as one patient said. "This was a tough topic, but Gigi took us from a dark place to smiles."

This is my wish for you. This has been life-changing for many people I have shared it with. That is my inspiration for writing this. I feel compelled to share this with as many people as possible. As I told my book coach, "I just can't keep it to myself!"

My husband Larry has been chanting the "write a book" mantra for several years, but finding time is a challenge and it was set in the back of my mind as an interesting idea. I have been speaking on the subject for years with positive feedback and given presentations on the therapeutic process I will be sharing here with you. After completing a professional training on my model in Prescott, Arizona several therapists echoed my husband's voice, "You should write a book!" and during this training I lost a dear friend and decided the time is **now**.

Section One is a guide to understanding grief and what you might experience on this journey. So many of us are new to this experience and feel lost and fearful as we begin to move into some of these emotions. Section Two is dedicated to *The Five Written Expressions of Grief* ™ and how to use this process to begin, continue and promote healing. The final section of the book is devoted to questions and answers common when grieving, focusing on the longer journey through grief. Most of us have questions we don't know who to ask or how to ask, still the questions continue to arise as we process our loss.

This is not a long book. I know that when I am grieving, I appreciate direction and support, but I don't have the energy or focus needed to read a big volume.

My goal is to help you to normalize the experience of grief and loss and assist in understanding the feelings and thoughts that come with it. I want to impart *The Five Written Expressions of Grief* ™ that can help you feel and move through difficult feelings while holding on to cherished memories. My intention is to help those who have not had the opportunity to grieve, those who feel lost, overwhelmed, stuck or are unable to find peace after a tragic loss.

After working with hundreds of patients using The Five Written Expressions, I am excited to share this with you and hope you find the relief and peace you are looking for as you move through the loss of a loved one.

"*Every Good Thing*"

~ GIGI

INTRODUCTION

Getting to the Other Side of Grief

Confused   Resentful

Overwhelmed   Lost

Empty   Numb

Depressed   Guilt   Angry

Lonely   Relieved

Shocked   Sad

Anxious

These are some of the feelings we have when experiencing loss. It can feel like a tornado, all these feelings surging upon you suddenly without any notice. Perhaps you are aware of the predicted storm; yet the feelings carry you away regardless. Surviving a loss can be challenging. Sometimes we go through this process naturally with little need of outside help, but many times that this is not the case.

As I work with clients, they may be very tentative at first, but then begin to feel safe and relaxed. That is when the questions start. I hear questions like "What should I be feeling?" "Will this pain last forever?" It was one of the reasons I decided to write a book. Several years ago, I was a keynote speaker on a cruise for a group of people in recovery from addictions. My

Husband came along. The night before I spoke about grief and loss he asked "Can I sit in on your presentation?" I was hesitant, but agreed, asking that he sit in the back row.

When I entered the room, he was seated in the front row, but I focused on my passion and message. After the presentation my husband stated "Now I really understand more about what you do." and acknowledged the reaction of the people in the room to what I shared about grief and *the Five Written Expressions of Grief* ™. He said "You really need to write a book!" I put it in the back of my mind as an interesting idea but could not see when I would have the time to sit, write and complete such a project.

I did, however, think of two particular clients who did some transformational grief work and decided I would contact them about this possible project to see if they would give permission for me to share their stories. I tucked this idea in the back of my mind as a "later-on project." I returned home and to work with a full schedule that next Monday. As I walked my last client out, sitting in the waiting room was one of these two people.

I had not seen Jason for counseling in more than five years. He would stop by my office near the anniversary of his recovery and thank me for helping him get started, but this was not that time of year. I greeted him and he said he felt he needed to see me, and I said I had planned to contact him. I shared this possible book project and asked if he would allow me to share some of his story and writings. He was touched and said I could use anything that would help other people as much as it had helped him. I took this as a sign from the Universe that a book was in my future.

I don't believe in coincidences, so here I am, writing. I considered what I wanted to impart to those who have lost loved ones and felt this book could help strengthen awareness and create comfort with an area of life that is often uncomfortable. Insights into what to expect as you go through the complicated process of grieving, can alleviate some of the confusion and overwhelm as you walk through so many thoughts, feelings and situations that are new to you. As I thought about Jason's' experience and what helped him, I felt it important to include normalizing the feelings and thoughts that you may have and highlighting our commonalities as well as uniqueness in grieving.

Section One of this book answers some questions, helps identify where you are in this process and creates a sense of control, or presents an ah-ha moment. Feelings come and go unexpectedly; finding something to grab on to, even the smallest thing, can help you feel more balanced and steadier. I have peppered the book with answers to questions about complications arising from your personal grieving style, the roles you gravitate toward when you are grieving and what gifts our loved ones left behind to accelerate healing and help ease the pain of loss. Overall, I want you to understand you are not alone, you and I are on a journey in this book where you can be open, vulnerable and think and feel about things that may leave you silent when it comes to sharing with others. This information will help return you to a normal footing and answer questions that come up consistently for those grieving.

The first section of the book builds a foundation preparing you for what, to me, is the most exciting and powerful part of the book, Section Two.

The Second Section of the book is dedicated to *The Five Written Expressions of Grief*,™ a healing process I developed over 25 years of working with clients, patients and their families. As I worked with clients and families, I noticed their sense of feeling stuck or overpowered by the intensity of their experience and at first felt helpless to assist. I thought there must be something I can contribute, so I began to create that something. The process has gone through changes and has been fine-tuned over the years until it seemed to be spot-on. *The Five Written Expressions of Grief*™ or what I call the *5 WE's*, have helped many who felt lost, stuck or alone in their journey toward healing.

I am excited to share this process with you, because I have witnessed its power and effect on many clients and patients over the last 25 years. The 5 WE's has helped hundreds of people find their way to peace after a loss by creating understanding, easing the pain, and releasing guilt, resentments and fears. Throughout the book I share stories from my personal and professional experiences to bring to life the connections that bind us as grievers.

My overall mission is to assist you in understanding, promote wisdom and reflection and provide a road map to move you through difficult feelings, to a more hopeful and peaceful space. My hope is that when you finish this book you will feel more comfortable with being in your grief and honor the feelings and thoughts as they come. Hope is a powerful feeling and can make the difference in our healing. You can and will get to the other side. This is not magical; there will still be pain, there will still be tough days but the dark clouds can part.

Peace.

The Grief Experience

Grief 101

Sarah was 45 when I met her. She found her way to counseling because of a sense of unrest. She was dissatisfied with her life and impatient with those around her. Her mood had gone from hopeful to apathetic about her future. For two years she had tried to figure this out on her own, to no avail. Working together, we found that a significant loss was at the core of her unrest.

Three years earlier Sarah lost her youngest son, Jay. He had been a happy child but a challenging teenager and young adult. Jay had trouble making decisions and fitting in. He tried drugs and alcohol, started and stopped school, and at some point gave in to his underlying depression. Sarah got a call one day informing her that Jay had taken his life.

Sarah's experience with unresolved grief is more common than we might think. Grief is a universal human experience, but it often goes unaddressed and we suffer alone. One in five of us will not reach 18 without significant loss in our lives. Losing a loved one, moving away from family, loss of health or feeling abandoned can each create a troubling sense of loss in us.

Sarah came to our second session armed with lots of questions. With the discovery that her unrest was related to losing her son, she wanted to know "everything." Her style of making sense of things in life was to ask questions to educate herself, then to apply her knowledge to her personal experiences. I agreed that knowledge is power. In any situation, the more we know, the less fear we tend to have. Understanding leads to greater awareness and increased ability to make healthy changes. We started with the basics.

What is Grief?

What do we mean when we speak of grief? Grief is our personal reaction to the experience of loss. Our experience of grief may include piercing, unfamiliar or unexpected emotions, thoughts and memories. Grief can color everything in our normal lives with sorrow, pain, disorientation, retrospection, and change. Often people are confused by these new feelings and thoughts. They may be unclear if they are experiencing grief or something different. To build a foundation of understanding we can begin with the word grief itself. One definition of grief is: "noun: deep sorrow, especially that is caused by someone's death."

As Sarah thought of her grief experience, she noted it was not just the feelings, but the way grief's impression coats and affects all aspects of her life. I explained that grieving goes beyond just the emotional process. It also affects us physically, mentally, spiritually, socially and culturally. As I introduced all the ways loss affects us, my clients and patients often find their experience makes more sense. Sometimes it is helpful and orienting to be aware of the wide realm that is the experience of grief.

In my workshops, I am often in a room with ten people, each with a different experience of grief. Sharing grief's frequency and variations helps them see how they are all connected. Often a patient will say, "That is my story, too" shifting the energy so everyone sees they are included in an epidemic of loss.

In the U.S. over 8 million people each year will suffer the loss of an immediate family member. An estimated 800,000 people lose their spouses each year, becoming widows and widowers. Approximately 1.2 million children will not be tucked into bed by a parent who is missing from their life. An estimated 104 fatal car accidents in the USA each day affect families and loved ones. It was with sorrow that I shared these statistics with Sarah, including the suicide rate in the USA, that now exceeds the number of fatal motor vehicle accidents each day, as loved ones surrender to depression, bullying, addiction, and other situations, feeling suicide is their best or only choice to end the pain.

Looking at grief in this way, we see that we are not alone as we mourn. At any time, someone else who is grieving is likely in your orbit. You are affected by their grief as they are affected by yours. As you think of family, friends, co-workers, and others who have influenced your life, you realize how much loss you have been touched by over the years. If we are not personally experiencing grief at this moment, we usually know someone who is in the midst of this kind of sorrow. One tragic loss of life can affect the many people who care about the deceased or their loved ones. Loss reverberates through our families, support systems, workplaces and communities. Every avenue of life is touched by the shift that loss provokes. Becoming aware of these interconnections helped Sarah feel less alone and more in touch with the universal community of people who grieve. It allowed her to see her commonalities and uniqueness as she related her life challenges to her grief.

The History of Our Understanding

As we continue to build on the foundation of understanding our grief experience, all roads for me start with Elizabeth Kubler-Ross. I call her our "Grandmamma" of knowledge about death, dying, grief, and loss. She was one of the first professionals to look at grief as a significant life event. Elizabeth, a Swiss-American Psychiatrist and Researcher, had a strong desire to study medicine that was unusual for women of her era.

During her Psychiatry residency in 1958, she was shocked by the treatment of dying patients. She began to host lectures, inviting both medical students and terminally ill patients to participate in conversations about death and dying. Elizabeth trained many physicians, students, and social workers over the next few years as she continued her research. Her study and observation of the emotions, feelings, and thoughts of terminally ill or dying patients led to her first book *On Death and Dying* in 1969 where she introduced *The 5 Stages of Grief.*

Even if you are unfamiliar with grief you may have heard of these famous five stages: shock and denial, sadness, anger, bargaining, and acceptance. These stages are the foundation of our understanding. Elizabeth Kubler-Ross opened the door and defined a framework from which to look at grief and death, maybe for the first time or at least in a different light.

This model had huge effects on society's awareness and comfort with the end of life. Kubler-Ross gave a great gift to the medical community as physicians began to really see their dying patients as still human, though fragile or suffering. She taught us we will all eventually be so affected and that patients can be comforted successfully during the last part of life by caring professionals and loved ones.

Her work and that of those following in her footsteps greatly influenced research in medicine and therapy, including her influence on me. Her five stages model helped me to identify what I was seeing in families and patients and increased my comfort level with my own feelings and those of patients. It made me think about how I could help others deal with anguish, anger, pain and sorrow.

In my practice, I saw many clients feeling stuck, overwhelmed, or paralyzed by grief. This accelerated my interest and desire to find a way of assisting my clients by helping them move through grief to healing. Thanks Grandmamma. I would not be me without you.

Why?

I occasionally hear, "Why do I need all this information about grief?" The answer is that this information leads to stronger understanding and helps make sense of your experiences of loss. It is the foundation leading to the next important step in this book: the work of actually processing your grief.

I look at processing grief as if it were a beautiful new house you want to build and live in. Some clients only want to talk about paint colors and landscaping, how they want the house to look when finished. But hard work is required to reach the result they want. They need to learn that the foundation is necessary. The house must be sited on your land and the foundation has to be poured. You cannot frame the house until the concrete is set and basic plumbing and electric are in place.

We can miss out on what is really important here, which is the journey, the work, or process that takes us to the new place we want to live. It is not just the end result; it is everything it takes to get us to that point. The growth is in the process, the reward is in the final result. You must go through this process step by step to build a strong foundation, a sturdy frame within which you can comfortably live. Then add the finishing touches that most please you and help create how you want your life to be.

That is the way of this book. I want to create a sturdy foundation for you to feel strong, make sense of some of the feelings and challenges of your grief, see how it affects you as a person in relation to others, and how you see your life, your future and the world. Once this is accomplished, you are ready to move to Section Two: *The Five Written Expressions of Grief*™ where we will, together, begin the work of healing.

Other Kinds of Loss

This book focuses on the permanent losses of loved ones through death, but I want to touch upon the impact of grief experienced from other losses. Many people I counsel are unaware of any link to grief in the struggles they have come to work through. Some elements of grief after losing a loved one apply to other forms of loss as there is a common thread in the feelings, struggles and healing process of grief. Feelings of grief and loss can occur when we are challenged with other difficult life events as well. We may feel loss when our best friend moves out of state, or when we retire from our job of twenty years, or when we become empty nesters as the last child goes off to explore the world and themselves. Maturing children may grieve the first time they leave home for any length of time. New jobs and opportunities can bring excitement and challenge, yet loss of the old and stepping into the new can also provoke a sense of loss.

Grief experience is unique to each person, and varies from event to event. We grieve losses from poor health, friendships we hoped would last a lifetime but did not, relationships, partnerships and marriages. We grieve moving away from family who have been around the corner and provided comfort and support. Many significant life changes stir up a sense of loss.

Even exciting changes can have grief trailing alongside. When we begin something new, we often leave something else behind that may have grounded us and made our world seem solid, stable, and safe. As we age, we can't do as much or do it as easily as we used to. Declining health is scary. Sudden changes and chronic health issues both can anchor overwhelming feelings of loss and fears of their impact on your ability to perform the simple tasks you take for granted, your abilities and independence. Loss of health may cause you to leave your job or retire, creating additional loss. Physical limitations may make us reliant on others for help, but many of us resist leaning on others and anguish about burdening loved ones.

Our sense of independence may be an additional loss. Like knocking over a line of dominoes: after the first one topples, the others follow. Feeling abandoned creates a severe sense of loss, a wound carried that can diminish our security and self-value.

Loss of a grounding relationship can cause sorrow: for example, loss of a parent by moving, death, or lack of attention and contact. Loss of a spouse, or long-time partner, best friend, or whomever you call your "rock" can shake your foundation.

We are a society of people on the move, but we need our grounding. Some of us do not like, and do not do well, with change. We fight it, we dig our heels in and rant about the new phone system at work or the move to a new town, school, home, or job. We toss and turn at night over the loss of our predictable environment, routine, and relationships. Change not only causes grief, it can be a major cause of stress. Even good, healthy, and exciting changes can cause stress. Getting married, buying your first house and becoming a parent are all things we may have dreamed of with excitement, but they come with a certain amount of stress.

So, loss of a loved one often ties into a string of losses. Loss of your loved one created an empty space in your life and heart, but some of the losses listed above may further the sense of instability and sorrow. If you are already off balance from change or other losses, you may not feel equipped to manage the additional pain of a loved one's loss.

Reflecting on the spectrum of loss, unpredictability, and multi-faceted grief, I felt compelled to write about COVID 19. It had been a century since the world had seen this kind of loss and grief, with most of us experiencing loss in so many areas of life. The pandemic provided fundamental lessons on humanity, fragility, love, and loss. The COVID 19 pandemic left an indelible impression on our communities, country, and society. This worldwide pandemic took us by storm, diminished our sense of safety and security, and left us fearful and untethered from our loved ones. We did not know what would happen next, or what information we would learn each day affecting if we could venture out of our homes.

Our way of life shifted to accommodate this deadly virus. Wearing a mask became a necessity. We had to distance ourselves from our loved ones, the very people who calm our fears and provide support. Touch has been underrated for a long time. When people could not reach out, take a hand, or give a hug, we saw how important human contact is, not only to our survival, but to our thriving and sense of well-being. Virginia Satir, a respected family therapist stated that we need four hugs a day for survival, eight a day for maintenance and twelve a day for growth.

Many of us who worked were isolated at home for a year or longer. In 2020 COVID was "breaking news" daily, and case numbers and deaths continued to climb in 2021 with over two hundred million cases worldwide. The loss of life was staggering. Worldwide over four million loved ones contracted the virus and did not survive. Global devastation left us in a continual state of grief. We lost parents, siblings, neighbors, friends, co-workers, grandparents, and dedicated medical providers who braved this scary environment to fight for the lives of our loved ones. We lost other essential workers, all brave souls, who checked out our groceries, taught our children, picked up our garbage, and drove our buses.

There was a helpless feeling as we did what we could, yet watched the numbers grow. We lost loved ones, but worse, we could not be there to hold their hands, wipe their tears, soothe their fears, and assure them that there is hope, and peace is coming. Humankind experienced an extended period of grieving as COVID 19 touched most of us personally. This State of Emergency caused increased isolation and disconnection, and led to increased depression. Anxiety and substance abuse skyrocketed, with only a small percentage of our isolated populations reaching out for and receiving help and support.

Society was compelled to change for the safety of ourselves and others, causing a sense of longing for the good old days when we could move freely around our cities and the world, show our smiles, be face-to-face, and comfort each other without hesitation.

During these long months, devastating loss of life was followed by sorrow and sadness. Society waited with hope for the collective sigh that comes with an end to a crisis. This pandemic was a foundational grief experience and, for some of us, the first time we may have had loss in our lives. It provided a fundamental lesson about grief and its long reach into our hearts and homes. It is in these experiences, these deep feeling, soul searching times, that the gifts of life and connection become crystal clear. I hope that families and friends were able to grieve and celebrate the lives of their departed loved ones, when time and conditions permitted them to once again, be together and mourn in healthy, healing ways.

CHAPTER 2

The Magic Question: Why People Come to Therapy

*"There is strength in
being open,
sharing
and trusting"*

~ GV

My first conversation with Jason was one of those phone calls I get periodically. "I need an appointment this week, or I have to move out of my house!" Jason's drinking had become unmanageable and his wife had given him an ultimatum: "Get help, or move out." To Jason's credit, he knew he needed help and was embarrassed that it took the fear of separation from his family to get it. The first step was a thorough assessment to define the seriousness of the problem.

When I asked him during our assessment appointment if he had experienced any significant losses in his life, his immediate answer was "No," followed by "Well yes... my Mother... but that was a long time ago..."

This question had taken Jason by surprise and required some thought before answering. The next thing I noticed was him beginning to flush and tear up. He became confused by what was happening to him at that moment. I was not confused; his grief was unresolved.

There are a handful of questions that I always ask a new client. One I call the "magic question." The magic question is, "Have you had any significant losses in your life?" This question has been the basis of many poignant moments in therapy. Even given all the statistics related to grief (and somewhat to my own surprise) I found about half *of the clients I do grief work with do not identify grief as an issue* when entering therapy.

Clients may not see how it affects their dissatisfaction, worries, and burdens until I ask that magic question. Sometimes when asked, their emotional reaction to the question surprises them. A lot of feelings have shown up over the years from people who thought they had grieved or "moved on," but instead, like Jason, were caught off guard by their own emotional response.

The length of time since a significant loss is not an indicator of acceptance or peace around that loss. Those of us who are "stuffers" internalize our sorrow, fears and worries, convincing ourselves the loss is "old history" or that we have dealt with it. The more time that has passed, the less we focus on our feelings and the more we focus on things more comforting or hopeful about the future.

When my client's eyes start leaking, or they become reflective, I know that grief is unfinished or unresolved. The client may have a traumatic grief experience that needs and wants to drift to the surface to be explored and addressed. Beyond the unexpected emotions, this question may present an "ah-ha" moment as pieces click together and people realize the shift in their lives or their discontent may have started around the time of a significant loss.

I routinely ask this question when I sit before a new client and asking is continually reinforced by their responses. We put grief in a box and wrap it up nicely (as if the box were not filled with sadness, pain, loneliness, or resentments.) Something in the back of our heads may say we are only "allowed" to feel this for some weeks or months, or that it is not okay to share these feelings with other people. Even worse, is the fear that no one else wants to hear about it.

We may feel no one wants to "really" know how we feel, so when asked, we give the auto response "Fine," and move on. When we are forthcoming and real with people, others may not notice we didn't give the traditional, "Fine, how are you?" response. Your response could be an opportunity to open up and share the reality of your experience. It can be difficult to say, "I am not okay," yet it is important to do so. You might debate if this is the right time to say something genuine or if this is the right person with whom to share your true feelings. We can be sure though that underlying grief does not just disappear when we ignore it, but will find its way to the surface and cause us problems.

Grief is not an isolated experience; it has a broad reach and can shape our foundation. A profound loss in one's life can stir up unanticipated questions, challenges, or pondering deep thoughts. You may not see things the same way you did in terms of importance and priorities. Grief can shape your thinking about your life, relationships and the future direction of your path. It is these ponderings and circumstances that lead clients to my door seeking some understanding.

Here are some areas of life that can be strained and stressed after the loss of a loved one. As you begin to reflect, you may see how grief and loss has mirrored your trials in life, impacting your overall functioning and stability. Loss may induce or heighten negative thoughts, behaviors, or reactions. Such events may have led; consciously or unconsciously, to you seeking professional help or guidance.

Relationships

Counseling may come later when underlying grief lingers in your heart and the back of your mind. Grief can be a constant compass that is influencing your life and relationships. You may check the temperature of a relationship, sometimes daily, evaluating and recalculating the significance, closeness, or distance that you feel. During this inventory, we may be quick or impulsive in deciding which relationships will strengthen and endure and others which have no clear place in the future.

There are those who may find their way to therapy to puzzle through issues with these old bonds. When we experience a loss, interactions with loved ones may become a bigger focus.

We may look at others around us and see them in a different light. Our perspective may lead to a pull to seek the comfort and support available to us, or fear the closeness of the relationship. We may become "clingy" as one man described his partner, or aloof, as if disinterested in others and their lives.

Feeling an intense bond is as natural a response as being fearful of being too close, with the risk of vulnerability. For true intimacy in a relationship, vulnerability is required. After a loss you may not be willing or able to put your soul out in this way, as it may trigger fear of losing closeness once again. In this way, we may prevent the very thing we want most, attachment. Such fear may show as you become more vague and superficial with your conversations and spend less time with those you care about. This dance of intimacy may lead to further disconnection and dissatisfaction in your relationships.

I am reminded of my client Kyle, he was painfully shy as a child and was finally at a time in his life where he was willing to take the leap, and risk closeness with, as he would say, his first *real* girlfriend, Bridget. That relationship opened his world and his shyness faded. But when Bridget was killed in a freak accident, he shut down and shut everyone off. He was determined not to let this happen to him again. He came to see me about his fears and loneliness.

Grief may show up as being "moody," impatient or irritable when you are around your support system. You may feel you cannot be yourself, prefer to be alone or unable to share what you are experiencing. From the outside it may look like disinterest in others. On the inside you may search to make sense of this reaction, as it does not feel like you are being your "old self."

We will discuss grief's other effects on relationships in Chapter 9, relating to some things that bring us peace and cause reflection.

Feelings

One man said to me, "I can't seem to express my feelings." Feelings can be tough for a lot of us. Some of us think we are not built to be touchy/feely. Others are comfortable with their emotional side. If you have gone through life thus far feeling neutral or staying in the slow lane with feelings, you may also be this way in grief. The opposite can also be true as well; when grieving we may experience feelings new to us or unrecognized within the reach of our recent memory.

Loss can be an awakening. Loss can shake us from the neutral path to embrace feelings that seem unfamiliar, uncomfortable, or tucked away and unfelt for months or years. You may have difficulty explaining to another what grief feels like for you. You may be unsure what you are feeling, and unable to identify this unfamiliarity, let alone explain it to others.

There seem to be two types of people: head types/thinking-focused and heart types/feeling-focused. I often repeat myself when asking one of my head type clients what they are *feeling* or how they feel about a particular issue. The reason for my repetition is that they first answer with what they *think*, as they are not used to speaking from a *feeling* place. My client Wyatt struggled with this issue. To help him make the connection, I asked him to close his eyes, take a deep breath and put his hand over his heart. "Now tell me how you *feel*."

Another avenue of angst when it comes to feelings may be when people say things like "I know how you feel," creating frustration and encouraging more isolation instead of an urge to open up. The truth is, no one can know exactly how you feel, even those with similar experiences. Each loss and the circumstances of that loss is unique, building a unique framework for how you move through your grief.

Some of our feelings can be very uncomfortable. Just dealing with them within ourselves is a challenge. Most of us are aware of feelings we are comfortable with, okay with, and then there are feelings we wish did not exist. It can be overwhelming to grieve and this may be the excuse you have been looking for to shut down. Sometimes the numbness of grieving causes lack of interest in other things and people, like a cloud that has moved over your life coloring everything gray. Feeling numb can be a comfortable place, not having to explore the overwhelming thoughts. You may have difficulty connecting with people who are important in your life without realizing why you keep them at a distance.

We tend to lean into feelings that make us feel safe and anchored while avoiding, sometimes like the plague, the ones that challenge our stability and create fear or a sense of loss of control. Yet it is important to find a way to identify, express and process what has been playing in your mind and tugging at your heart.

We lean into feelings that make us feel safe and anchored but avoid those that challenge our stability, create fear, or a sense of loss of control. If your intent is to skirt or skip feelings, this will not lead you to the peace you seek. "The healing is through the feelings" has become my mantra. The route of stuffing your feelings may be a road you can take, but it is unlikely to bring you to a place of comfort. Solid, non-judgmental support can help you to open the door to understand, express and process your feelings, leading to continual healing.

Interesting Fact

Research on "Broken Heart Syndrome" provides evidence that extreme stress caused by grief or other shocking life events can lead to a reaction where the body releases stress hormones causing a small part of the heart to briefly swell and stop beating.

~ Reference American Heart Association, 2017, December 12 article "Is broken heart syndrome real?"

"The healing is through the feelings"

~ GV

Distancing

After loss, you might find you prefer to be alone with your thoughts and feelings to sort things out. However, that may distance you from your support system. Or, your personality may encourage you to reach out, and share your thoughts and feelings.

One of the hurdles to being open is that some people may not know what to do or say, so they may say nothing or take the lead in distancing. This may be the easiest way for them to manage their discomfort. They may not want to make a mistake by doing or saying the "wrong thing". Loss will change you; others may notice you are just not yourself. They may even say this directly. One interpretation is that the person is trying to understand what is wrong.

There are also fixers out there! They want you to be okay, back to your old smiling happy self, and will try anything to help you get there. Another point of view is that people may be uncomfortable with you acting as you are now. That may make you more self-conscious about your behavior or encourage you to put on an act to ease the discomfort of others. It may take more energy than you can access to deal with others' discomfort without being disloyal to yourself and your feelings.

When we distance ourselves from others, we may feel safer. If you have experienced multiple losses, distancing may seem like refuge or a protective barrier, as your soul cannot imagine the pain of losing another person of significance in your life.

Mental Health Impact

Counseling can help ease or manage symptoms of the depression, anxiety, and fearfulness that can keep you up at night. Those who have already experienced long-term depression know the challenge of managing everyday life, but now have the added loss of a loved one to further unsettle their mood. Depression can be exacerbated by loss, as loss carries its own form of sadness which deepens depression.

If it is already hard to get up and find motivation each day, or your thinking leans toward sad thoughts, lacking hope and optimism, such thoughts and feelings may increase. Approximately 10-15% of people have a "severe" reaction to grief and chances of a severe reaction are very high for people struggling with depression prior to their loss.

Mood shifts can create thoughts that the world is unpredictable, or cause intrusive thoughts, and feelings of being lost as you navigate through challenges and decisions. This unpredictability is reinforced by unanticipated loss. Depression can take the form of disinterest, withdrawal or the disconnection that I wrote of earlier.

Those already struggling with anxiety may become even more fearful. We live in a world requiring us to be on the alert. This "alert" can display as anxiety that makes our minds race, and our bodies restless. We think of all the possible situations. "What else will happen?" "Who's next?" "Could it be me?" "Does this disease run in our family?" These thoughts can create more fear and sleepless nights.

Anxiety can lead to over-analyzing, running scenarios through your head or on paper. Anxiety creates a need to be in control or in charge of something...or anything. Reaching for control provides a sense of relief that you are at least doing something. I encourage "Doing" as a key for those with anxiety or depression because it creates movement, produces results, and feels stabilizing.

Many grieving clients have new anxiety about death, fears about their physical health or the health of those they love. This is often stuffed deep down and people have a hard time opening up about this fear. They may not have had this fear before because life felt predictable before a loved one left a hole that cannot be filled or replaced.

This fear is common. Some dream that something is wrong with another loved one or themselves. This fearfulness is more common for those who already had anxieties. However, many people with anxiety have not had this specific fear prior to the loss of a loved one. Anxiety may have been previously restricted to things that felt like "real" possibilities or a specific avenue of life. A significant propellant of 'death anxiety' can be related to your world spinning out of control. The sense that I am not in control and the reality of how quickly an ordinary day can turn into an unspeakable tragic loss, feeds anxiety. Fearing death and the anxiety that accompanies it, are stuffed and not shared with other people out of concerns of being labeled as "odd" or "crazy" or falling out of the "normal" reaction expected by others.

Some fear that embracing such thoughts means "I am losing it" or, even worse, speaking out would make these thoughts real and would lead to something bad happening. If you have not sought assistance with anxiety or depression, this may be the time to start. Particularly if these thoughts are intrusive and persist for weeks or longer and/or disrupt your life, I encourage you to seek help from a Psychiatrist, Therapist or Primary Care Physician. This book is a supplement to help you understand, explore and begin healing through grief. The book may also illuminate issues leading to an additional step or need for more support. I have a strong belief in "mental hygiene." Chronic mental dis-ease is a real and important health crisis in our society and deserves proper attention.

If these anxieties and mood shifts are new to you, in early grief this reaction is normal. After a loss you may find the more you talk about it to caring people you trust, the more you will hear from others who have similar feelings, dreams and thoughts. In my practice and workshops, I see this repeatedly and the relief can almost be felt in the air.

Depression, anxiety, disconnection and relationship problems, may have been present for a while, but become unmanageable after a loss. A sense of feeling lost and needing direction with career or personal goals also drives people to look for help and guidance.

When we struggle with grief, our sadness can turn to depression, our fears can lead to more anxiety, or a period of reflection may cause upheaval. Unidentified grief and loss can lead to restless nights and people reach out for help for inability to sleep or discontent in various areas of life. Difficulty managing moods can also be a motivator to seek assistance. Sleep can be challenging when your mind is racing with memories, happy or sad, or with "What's next?" questions.

Existential Crisis

Juanita started her day as usual on automatic pilot. But as she looked in the mirror, she *really* saw herself and muttered "When did this happen? "She noticed drooping eyes and jowls forming around her jaw. She was 64, one year away from Medicare and two years younger than her brother Raul who passed away suddenly in a boating accident. The sparkle of youth had left her eyes, replaced by wisdom and reflection.

None of us know how much time we have on earth. Aging and loss remind us of this fact. As we age, we can't do as much or do it as easily as we used to. There are more trips to the doctor and other reminders of our maturing bodies. We may realize there is no time like the present to get healthy and live fully. This may be our new mantra. You may add doctor's appointments to the to-do list, inspect your body for changes or start an exercise regimen.

You may not notice that the emotional experience that led you to counseling started with a loss that shifted understanding of who you are, your roles, or your place in the world. Areas of life that seemed certain and grounding prior to loss, may now be full of questions and uncertainty. As we look around us and become more aware, we realize we are in constant transformation. Loved ones, careers, communities are in a steady path of change.

Mental health may climb up the list of your priorities. Anxiety or depression may spike or be exacerbated while grieving. That was the case for Oliver. He had struggled with life balance and mental well-being in the past, but after his recent loss things seemed to go upside down. Without his mentor, Raymond, he felt lost, uncertain about where he was going in life, and hesitant to make decisions or changes, so he called me for guidance.

You may feel this is the time for a helpful and objective ear to sort through life goals, purpose or general mental hygiene. There is a new awareness driving you toward living.

Substance Use

Another reason clients seek counseling or treatment is for alcohol or substance abuse. Clients already struggling with addiction may link increased use to a death or say something like, "When my brother died, that's when I really fell off the rails." I have heard this over and over again. Addiction in our country is a crisis. We lose many beautiful, struggling people each year to this disease. Often, secondary or underlying issues contribute to pushing people into, or deeper into, addictive behaviors.

Loss can be a traumatic experience. We all look for a way to cope, but the way we find may be healthy or unhealthy. Some who were social drinkers or occasionally used substances may find comfort in continued or increased use to numb out or to be in touch with feelings after a loss. I hear statements like, "The only time I could bear to think about my mother was when I was altered." This also meant the only time they were able to "feel" about their mother was when they were altered. Then there is the opposite: "The only time I could escape my thoughts and feelings was when I was drinking." Change can cause us to reach for substances to help us navigate the stress, sense of loss, and overwhelming feelings it brings.

Most of us like life to be predictable and some would prefer for it to lean toward boring or status quo: no waves, clear sailing, no unpleasant surprises, no drama. Even small changes in life can throw those struggling with substance abuse off kilter, so imagine what losing someone important in your life can do. Claire's world became off balance when she lost her sister Marie. They were very much alike, except that Claire fell into addiction and Marie did not. While Marie struggled with a chronic illness, Claire's use of alcohol and drugs picked up. After Marie was laid to rest, Claire lost herself and all her feelings to her addiction. Substance use is a coping method easy to slip into; it is just not a helpful one. And it comes with a string of other serious consequences including additional losses.

When I do grief workshops at inpatient mental health/ substance abuse facilities, I read a list of statements and ask that everyone in the group stand if their answer is yes. When I read " One of my primary reasons for being in treatment is grief and loss," half of the group or more usually stand. All and all, the magic question presents an opportunity for immediate acknowledgment of unresolved loss, a starting point for self-reflection, new insights, and the release of bottled-up feelings. This question has yet to let me down. :)

The Power of Loss

Why is grief important? Grief is one of the most common experiences we have in life. We cannot turn on the television without hearing about some recent tragedy in our neighborhoods, in our city, across the country or in the world. For this reason, I stopped watching local news in my city for almost two years when I worked in a prominent trauma-one neurological center. It became unbearable to turn on the news and see what tragic event would await me the next day on top of the general sense of sadness these experiences induced.

All this loss has a huge impact on our general well-being, our mental health, addiction issues, and progress in healing from other traumatic history. Millions of individuals already struggling with depression, anxiety and other forms of emotional overload may become more unstable under added pressures of grief and decreased ability to focus on self-care. They may not reach out to their support systems or lack support to turn to. Our symptoms may worsen. Inability to focus and concentrate may paralyze us.

Those with substance dependency or other addictions may act out or relapse to their chosen addiction, relying on their old primary coping skills to help them numb out, cope with uncomfortable feelings and situations or feel in touch with those feelings. Traumatic history can be triggered.

Perhaps another loss that is unresolved or remains fresh in memory will occupy our thoughts, emotions, and energies. It is common to think of other loved ones you have lost at this time, especially if you were not present at the time to grieve that loss. Not only are you grieving for the person you recently lost, but sometimes multiple other losses from the past.

We minimize losses from the past. The longer the period of time that passes, the more we feel "time has healed it." The subject of grief and loss often produces fear or discomfort for people. We shy away from talking about it and struggle with what to say and how to help and comfort our friends and family going through a loss.

Me After You

*Mourning is like losing the sunrise,
each dawn coming without the light,*

*All life painted in hues of gray,
following me,
thoughts of you abound,
everything I see a reminder,
rich in memories,*

*You completed my scene and turned
ordinary to awe and
uh, how I miss life with you.*

BY GIGI VEASEY

CHAPTER 3

What to Expect When Grieving

The first call came on Wednesday July 9th, 2014 around 6:30 pm from my friend LJ. "Hi LJ!"

Monica and LJ were on vacation in Maui. The message I had received earlier in the day from LJ had asked me to give him a call. The last time LJ called me was for a recipe, so I wasn't anticipating any urgency.

Now as we spoke, he said something more than surprising. Monica, his wife and my close friend, was in a hospital with heart trouble, and they were taking her into surgery. "WHAT??" I repeated this several times. LJ said he'd call me when she was out of surgery. We both took an optimistic view that she would be okay, but she was probably in for some significant recovery time. At the time of LJ's call I was packing the car to leave for Prescott, Arizona to run a nine-hour training for a group of therapists entitled "Surviving A Loss" (ironic).

I proceeded with the training, with positive thoughts in my head. I texted LJ the next morning at 8:53am to check in; I hadn't slept well and was worried. He relayed that they were at the hospital late and she hadn't woken up yet. "Hopefully sometime today she will," he sent at 10:12am. The next text at 2:09pm attempted to shake me out of my denial "Not good news, major strokes. May not survive." WHAT?!! I became disoriented, emotionally overwhelmed with repeated episodes of feeling numb and heavy. "This just couldn't be happening! Monica is young; only 52, healthy and on vacation in Hawaii for heaven's sake!"

On July 11th, LJ texted me with an update. I called him, and learned the MRI had verified severe damage to both sides of Monica's brain.

This is when the pain in my own heart became overwhelming. No more denial; this was fatal. We talked and cried and talked. Family was on the way.

I shared what I was experiencing with the therapists in the training group. I couldn't have asked for a more empathic, well-trained group to help me through and understand what I was experiencing. By the next morning my head was swirling with just one word, "WHY??" and some anger kicked in as I repeated to myself, "Of all the people,... so young... so good and beautiful inside and out... so much to live for and share with us all ... she has been taken away from us!"

It was clear to me now; she would not survive and it would be soon. I thought about her wonderful life, her friends and family, and what my life would be like without my dear friend of over 25 years.

I was grateful it was quick, no suffering, and she was in Hawaii, her favorite place on the earth.

This is when I decided to write this book. I began writing immediately.

On July 13th, 2014 the text simply read "TOD 11:38AM"

Grieving Signs

This was only the beginning of my journey through grief. There were many more days, weeks and months to come as I bounced back and forth through a confusing mix of emotions, thoughts and physical symptoms.

Symptoms of grief are as broad as a sea. The word "symptom" is defined as an indication, sign or warning sign. Dr. Elizabeth Kubler-Ross gave us a foundation to guide us and explained that we can expect to experience five stages of grief: shock/denial, sadness, anger, bargaining and acceptance. As a clinician and grief expert, throughout my story of loss, I recognized all these stages. But to the untrained, these emotions may be unexpected and feel confusing, overwhelming, even random.

For me, shock, denial and disbelief came quickly as this tragic loss unfolded. I wanted to push it away, but as reality settled into me, I felt the intensity of my sadness, a sadness that stuck with me for many months and years. I had been so angry at the unfairness of losing Monica who had been so young and vital. We had many plans to continue growing and sharing life experiences together. I spent many days wrestling with the "why?" of bargaining and how I wanted to wish this away as a bad dream or an awful joke. There were times when I settled into my acceptance that she was gone and that this was permanent. I continued to flow through these thoughts and feelings again and again as birthdays, gatherings, and as other events stirred up my grief once again.

We can add an exhaustive list of how these grief feelings show up in life with no order or predictable intensity. Many other feelings and thoughts will be a part of this journey through grief as well. We are all unique individuals; how we feel varies from person to person, from loss to loss. Circumstances shift with each loss as does our responses and the intensity of the feelings we experience.

There are many components and questions around grief that shape our display of emotion. Were you close? Distant? Present at the time? Were you just moving through another earlier loss? Were you already struggling emotionally? Was the death a peaceful exit from life or a harsh one? I could go on and on. The answers to these questions all help construct our unique response to grief. The path may feel at times unpredictable or random and at other times comforting and stabilizing.

I will share some common feelings, thoughts, and reactions to grief that you can compare to your own grief experience.

"The depth of our grief is
in line with the
depth of our connection"

~ GV

Overwhelmed

You may feel overwhelmed, perhaps outside of your usual self. Some describe feeling almost paralyzed by their grief. Overwhelming feelings may cause you to be temporarily disoriented, unable to recall words or names you have known for years. You may be forgetful about fundamental habits and activities. The sense of feeling overwhelmed can be purely emotional or have a physical aspect. There may be a sense of meandering or being almost detached from yourself. You may be tearful at unexpected times and have difficulty controlling your emotions. This occurs more frequently right after a loss, as your body needs a chance to adjust. My client Justine described this. As she was telling me a story, she lost track of what she was saying and at the end of the session was searching for her sunglasses that were on her head.

When I refer to "the body" as in the paragraph above, I mean to include all aspects of our existence that come to play as we grieve: physical, mental, emotional and spiritually. Things you have done every day for the last twenty years may now seem impossible to manage. Your focus and attention may be impaired as your routine in life is disturbed. Physical exhaustion from grief may set in, leaving no stamina for productivity. You may not feel mentally sharp and your spiritual beliefs may be tested. Grief is a process; and as you go through this journey, your whole being is affected.

Sadness, Anxiety & Addiction

Sadness may come in the form of feeling "down, "crying or lethargy. Sadness is part of grief. Another component of sadness in grieving is a physical heaviness, a feeling like you are carrying something heavy around with you, something that slows you and causes you to lumber around as days pass. Even after a peaceful night's rest, you may feel fatigued upon awakening. Or sleep may elude you. You might get two hours or six, but regardless you remain exhausted. You may toss and turn, restlessness taking over your body, not just your mind. Keith is an example of this. After his wife's death he came for counseling. One day he said he had not slept through the night in weeks. He was fearful of the toll this would take on his ability to return to work and also care for his two small children.

Anxiety in grief may show up as your mind racing but going nowhere, as though your foot is pressing down hard on the gas pedal while your car is in park. Thoughts come and go, sometimes at high speed as you review what you know, what happened, ask questions about what you don't know, evaluate the strength of love in your relationship and so forth. Sitting still may seem impossible or uncomfortable. You may notice a need to "do something;" your body might want and need to take action to heal the helpless heart.

If you were depressed prior to your loss, or you have a tendency to be anxious or a "worrier," it can be challenging to be emotionally present, but presence is considered a necessary foundation of effective grieving.

As a griever struggling with significant mental and emotional stability, you may not be emotionally available or grounded to shoulder a loss. Loss while feeling unstable can lead to heightened symptoms of present depression, anxiety, or helplessness. A complicated or overwhelming life has just become even more so with the knowledge of the loss of a loved one. Numbness may seem the best option and you may shut down emotionally or even search for this numbness by self-medicating with alcohol, medications or even food.

The goal being to avoid the reality of the traumatic experience by folding into yourself and detaching from a reality too painful to deal with on top of daily struggles of managing your mood. This may look like a lack of caring from those on the outside, but it is self-preservation.

In my many years of working with adults struggling with alcohol and drug addictions, I have seen people in recovery relapse under the strain of loss, or report that their drinking or substance use intensified after the loss of their loved one. This story is not uncommon, with grief not initially identified as the trigger that caused the relapse or change in pattern of use of the substance. Struggling with mental health and/or substance use necessitates priority, which means grieving may take place months, or even years down the road after stability returns. Grieving may be initiated by treatment sought for other issues or encountering a new loss that triggers past losses and pulls older memories and feelings to the surface. It is then that healing can begin.

Pain

For some, the pain of grief can unhinge the griever. Such pain can be staggering. It can feel like it might swallow you whole. It may feel intolerable and those who suffer may question if they can survive its intensity. Pain can drive people to feel like they no longer want to be among the living as it is too much to bear. It can be difficult to envision yourself getting beyond the intensity and sorrow that create feelings of helplessness or hopelessness.

Those engulfed by this kind of painful grief may wish that they were the one who passed away instead of their loved one, or may have magical thinking about taking the place of their beloved. Physical and emotional pain may merge to seem as one. The old saying "There is a fine line between physical and emotional pain" seems to be true. Looking at how emotional pain affects our bodies; the symptoms are similar. One client told me he thought he was "coming down with something." I said "Yes, you may be coming down with grief."

Tragic loss also affects our immune systems (as any major stressor can do) and can lead to compromised health. Our bodies are amazing machines. During a stressful emergency or traumatic event, our bodies are highly efficient. As stress lessens or settles, our bodies begin to show delayed effects including pain. Some grievers may need medical assistance with existing physical ailments, anxiety, depression or sleep disturbance created or exacerbated by prolonged pain of grief. It will take time and patience to return to a normal life.

> *"Distraction is a helpful coping skill for physical and emotional pain"*
>
> ~ GV

Progression

The progression of grief is not what you might expect. You may have thoughts drifting around in your head that say, "Each day will get a little easier." Recovering from the loss of a loved one is not like a cold or flu where you feel it coming on, brace yourself, suffer through the intensity of the illness, and look toward the slow but steady progression that returns you to good health. Grieving doesn't follow the predictable pattern of getting a little better each day until you feel yourself again. The natural course of grieving is two steps forward, one step back, eventually leading to more forward days than slide-back days.

Families and loved ones struggle with this progression, as good days bring a sense of relief and hope, followed by disappointment when getting hit with another overwhelming day. Once you discover this pattern, it can make you wary of good days and fearful of letting hopes rise. It may be hard to find a balance between living with hope versus fear of more slide-backs. This is one of the challenges faced by grievers and was one of my greatest challenges as a new social worker in the hospital.

I spent the first week of my hospital internship with my hand covering my mouth in intense distress repeating how shocked, horrified and sad I was for each patient as I heard their stories of illness and imminent loss. After a week of this, I had an "ah-ha" moment of my own. I realized that I could not help the patients if I remained in a state of my own overwhelm. The solution was simple. Find a balance between being overwhelmed and being caring, empathic, present, and attentive. This change allowed me to advocate and take action on the patient's behalf. It was a steep hill to climb, but it was what I needed to do to make life better for my patients.

I recall my good friend Nora's grief after the anticipated loss of her husband. There were times when she would be overwhelmed, sad, and angry, with a mixture of other feelings. Without notice, a day would arrive where she felt that "I think I am finally making progress and moving through this grief and pain." Only to find herself in the coming days pulled back to where she had started with her feelings. Stepping forward and sliding back continued for a year. She was tentative when the time arrived where she again landed on acceptance. This time, her acceptance did not falter, and feelings of peace and normalcy slowly returned to her life.

When you have a loved one in the hospital, riding the waves from hopefulness to feeling deflated as their condition improves or deteriorates, can be especially difficult. As you sit with them during visiting hours one day, you find them sitting up, recognizing you and maybe taking sustenance for the first time in days. Your heart swells with hope and joy. But when you return the next day, they are down again, possibly non-verbal, restless and struggling. This up and down is painful to watch and emotionally draining as you never know what to expect next from each day on the emotional roller coaster. This up and down progression is the same after the loss of life. Eventually, after months or years, you will find your normal footing returning or that a new normal has arrived.

"Grief is not a competitive sport"

~ GV

Stuffing of Feelings

Some people deal with grief by stuffing feelings. Perhaps this is the way you have dealt with emotional situations in the past, your "go-to" way of handling life when things get complicated. Harboring these deep feelings does not vanish them. They only wait in dark corners of your mind and heart until you are ready to face and release them. Stuffing is to be avoided. It is a direct road to becoming stuck in your grief.

I see the body as a container. It can hold a multitude of memories, experiences and feelings. However, the body only has so much room and if we hold on or ignore thoughts and feelings, they can make this amazing body of ours ill. This illness can come in many different forms. You might feel physically ill, becoming clumsy, bumping into things or dropping things as your body tries to manage the stress of containing all you are going through. There is a mental aftermath to stuffing. You might struggle with remembering basic things, forgetting words and appointments. Stuffing can lead to emotional outburst, pushing loved ones away, or misdirected emotion all without conscious awareness of what the outburst is really about. All and all, grief finds a way to the surface.

Your body will let you know when it has taken in all the stuffed feelings, overwhelming thoughts and misdirected anxieties it can tolerate. Pay attention. Be inquisitive about feelings and situations, turn your thoughts inward and ask if you are stuffing thoughts and feelings. Are you sharing your pain and getting the support you need to move toward healing? Carlos made a point of telling me during his first session, "No offense, but I don't really believe in this counseling thing...it was a last resort." I told him I didn't mind being his last shot at peace. :)"

It can be difficult for those used to handling things on their own and sucking it up. It is okay. It is acceptable to need help with the pain of grief. Asking for help may be foreign to you, as your style has been to stand on our own and work through it solo. Asking for help is not a sign of weakness, it is a show of strength. It takes a lot of self- reflection, courage, and energy to admit you cannot handle something on your own. Take the hand reaching out to you. It does not mean you are not strong or capable. It only means that you are human.

*"You can't shut off
the faucet
and think there
is no more water"*

~ GV

Expressions of Emotion

Leave room for all your feelings, not just the easy or loving ones. Each of us has a mental list of feelings we are willing to show, express, and share. Most of us would like to stay in the sunshiny feelings, making everything look like we are good, hopeful, getting better and finding peace. I call these butterfly and rainbow feelings. We also have the thunderstorm feelings of pain, fear, anger, hurt, and resentment. These feelings are real and just as necessary to express when we are grieving. Anger may show up, and we may choose to express it as a way to feel in control or powerful. Most often, anger harbors fear, hurt, or both. Look beyond the face of anger to hidden feelings below the surface. Ask "Am I feeling fear or hurt?" If the answer is yes, address the fear or hurt directly. Others may choose anger to fight off sadness and tearfulness that we might be misjudged as weakness. I feel the strongest thing you can do is show genuine emotion.

Few of us have had a purely rosy path in our lives and relationships without "speed-bumps" along the way. These speed bumps may cause regret, resentment or guilt. If you have a spotless relationship, you are blessed and your path to healing will likely be easier. Leave room for ALL your feelings, not just the easy or lovely ones. I encourage people to express "the good, the bad and the ugly" of their grief. All feelings are necessary and what we feel is never wrong, it just is. This may be an opportunity to begin to know yourself on a deeper, emotional level.

"Feeling is a step forward,
not a step backwards"

~ GV

Support System

We need support and thrive when we feel supported, cared for, and loved while going through the overwhelming experience of loss. Absence of a support system, (family, friends, partner...), can leave you feeling alone with grief. Loss of a loved one can either pull a family/support system together, or create more distance. Past conflicts may suddenly be unimportant or swept away in the midst of a crisis. It may surprise you how unimportant past bickering, and unkind words become when tragedy has struck your family. Past conflicts may simply fall away, leaving a foundational desire to be close, and connected to those who truly understand the sense of loss you are experiencing.

A loss could have the opposite effect. Conflicts could hold fast, or even intensify, as old history comes to the surface. If there were hard feelings about childhood traumas, unresolved disagreements or strained communication, these patterns might be heightened. I have seen the best and the worst sides of people during this time of stress, sadness, pain and loss. Docile, calm, easy going personalities turn to raging or controlling behaviors and the opposite as well. Those bent on making things difficult for everyone involved may settle in and show their most caring and loving selves. It is a mystery, perhaps unpredictable, how you will react and behave when the time comes to grieve.

You may experience the loss of the person who was the foundation of your support system, the one that was always there to listen and support you. Losing this connection can shake up your world; another cannot take your loved one's place. It might feel like a betrayal to lean on someone else in your loved one's absence. Building new bonds may be challenging and take time as you navigate this process.

The topics of grief and death are difficult to talk about, even when support is present, there may be a tendency to not want to "burden" anyone with the need to share feelings. Those with good, strong support systems don't always reach out to them, even knowing they will be met with warmth, and understanding. If your goal is to avoid burdening those who care for you, dump this goal and run for the help and comfort you need! Many grieving people would, in a second, reach out to help someone else, without hesitation, yet have not figured out that it is okay to receive. Grievers who seek the comfort of someone who understands and makes them feel safe to grieve are ahead of the game. Healing begins when you share your thoughts and feelings.

The Why??

"WHY??" is **The** gnawing question we have when experiencing loss. There are so many "why" questions and they begin immediately after someone becomes ill or dies. We want to know why. We need to know! Our brains kick into overtime trying to make sense of a tragedy. We can become preoccupied with the puzzle pieces and the details of what led to this loss. We are driven to search for answers. We question everyone involved, from those present at the time of tragedy to the physician who delivered the bad news. We question weather conditions on the road before the accident, test results, health status and care given. We are driven to know the reasons.

This continues as we turn to "Why them?" "Why now?" or "Why is this happening to me and/or them?" The questions burn a pathway in our brains asking "How can I make sense of what I am experiencing?" The need for control is an attempt to steady ourselves. As with many things in life, the more we know and understand, the less fear we have. Yet, unlike other events, loss sometimes presents a situation where we will never have all the answers. The "why" avenue is where people can get stuck in their grief. Some of us just flat out refuse the idea that there are no answers. Even if you were to get those answers, they may not make you feel any more at peace. Elizabeth Kubler-Ross would call this an example of the bargaining done around grieving. I describe bargaining as "what if, what if, I wish, I wish." Wanting things to be different, to be able to wave a magic wand and change the circumstances so that one decision, turn, word, event would lead down a different path in which this tragedy did not occur. Going further down this thought track we succumb to second guessing our actions and ourselves. "I should have done more, given more, called more, pushed more..." again with the goal of an alternate outcome.

These thoughts are used to evaluate our responsibility, or what kind of mother, brother, friend was I to this person when they were here? We can beat ourselves up over not doing enough or having enough presence in our loved one's life. McKenzie struggled with these issues. She was extremely close to her brother Maxwell. They had been inseparable until he went off to college. Although they talked and texted often, she missed any signs that he was not feeling well and was in denial. When Max passed away a year later from cancer, McKenzie told me she had spent hours reviewing every text he sent, looking for a hint of a problem she should have picked up on.

This vein of thinking creates an assumption that we can foresee the future. Hindsight is always spot on. But none of us know when it will be the "last time." The last time we talk, see each other, laugh, argue, travel, support and comfort one another.

In Limbo

Expect periods of time where you are "in limbo," not necessarily feeling good or happy, but not feeling overly sad and down. It is an in-between station. This may be comfortable or a bit disturbing. If someone asks how you are doing or feeling, you might say "I am not really sure... or I don't know, or I guess okay..."

Eric had spent months in limbo before he came to see me. He said he was feeling guilty, yet relieved about not feeling more. We discussed removing the pressure as his caring and love for his best friend Andrew was not in question. Being in Limbo may feel peaceful, as if you are taking a break from heavy feelings of grieving. You might feel numb, as if you cannot tune in or you are out of touch with feelings temporarily. Sometimes numbing is a necessary respite from the intensity of the feelings you have been emoting and carrying. The pendulum does not always swing from misery to joy. It might reset at this midpoint. This may lead to feeling guilty, questioning if you are not feeling enough, not experiencing the 'required' amount of pain as a griever. This is when we begin to judge ourselves, measuring some self-determined line indicating we are not doing it right or avoiding our grief all together. It's okay to rest here. Your body needs time to recuperate and process this occurrence. I give you permission to just BE for a while and catch your emotional breath.

The Day-to-Day Emotional Journey

Other variances on this journey include the day to day, sometimes morning to evening shifts in emotions. This may be an unanticipated happening. Some of us find the most difficult part of the day is first thing in the morning. We wake and become newly aware once again that we are alone, or that another dawn has come without the one we love to share it with. Morning solitude can increase the feeling of being alone or stuck in your thoughts before the activities of the day can come along to distract you. Mornings for others come forth with feelings of hopefulness and purpose. Ready for another day of purposeful work and contact with others to fill the gap in life as we continue toward resurrecting our normal routines. Mornings and evenings tend to be the biggest challenges. Evenings can be more difficult for some of us. Days may seem manageable because we have been busy, but when evening comes and the world quiets, we may feel more alone and our thoughts may turn back to our grief.

Bennet struggled with evenings. He and his wife Meg had been together for over 30 years and when the world quieted, he felt lost without her questions, curiosity, and laughter in the house. The more your loved one was a part of your daily routine, the more difficulty you may have moving forward as so many environments, belongings and activities remind you of what once was. Evenings are also quiet times when we may have had quality time from our busy jobs and households to finally be present with our loved one and share the joys and challenges of the day or enjoy the silent comfort of just being near. If you are retired and most of your time was spent with your loved one, this can be tough. Most of your time and attention may have been centered around your partner and the routine you both so easily moved through. Don't neglect the other loves in your life. Extended family and close friends can distract you and prevent you from becoming isolated.

Sleep can be a welcomed distraction from the reality and heavy feelings of grief. Sleep can also be a way to hide or avoid, so be honest with yourself about your motives.

*"Grief carries a vacancy,
and we can either fill it
or sleep through it"*

~ GV

The Old Guy

I found this on-line some time ago, a young woman looking for some guidance after she lost a friend and did not know what to do or how to grieve. This "Old Guy's" response seems to sum up all that I am trying to impart.

Alright, here goes. I'm old. What that means is that I've survived (so far) and a lot of people I've known and loved did not. I've lost friends, best friends, acquaintances, co-workers, grandparents, mom, relatives, teachers, mentors, students, neighbors, and a host of other folks. I have no children, and I can't imagine the pain it must be to lose a child. But here's my two cents.

I wish I could say you get used to people dying. I never did. I don't want to. It tears a hole through me whenever somebody I love dies, no matter the circumstances. But I don't want it to "not matter." I don't want it to be something that just passes. My scars are a testament to the love and the relationship that I had for and with that person. And if the scar is deep, so was the love. So be it. Scars are a testament to life. Scars are a testament that I can love deeply and live deeply and be cut, or even gouged, and that I can heal and continue to live and continue to love. And the scar tissue is stronger than the original flesh ever was. Scars are a testament to life. Scars are only ugly to people who can't see.

As for grief, you'll find it comes in waves. When the ship is first wrecked, you're drowning, with wreckage all around you. Everything floating around you reminds you of the beauty and the magnificence of the ship that was, and is no more. And all you can do is float. You find some piece of the wreckage and you hang on for a while. Maybe it's some physical thing. Maybe it's a happy memory or a photograph. Maybe it's a person who is also floating. For a while, all you can do is float. Stay alive.

In the beginning, the waves are 100 feet tall and crash over you without mercy. They come 10 seconds apart and don't even give you time to catch your breath. All you can do is hang on and float. After a while, maybe weeks, maybe months, you'll find the waves are still 100 feet tall, but they come further apart. When they come, they still crash all over you and wipe you out. But in between, you can breathe, you can function. You never know what's going to trigger the grief. It might be a song, a picture, a street intersection, the smell of a cup of coffee. It can be just about anything... and the wave comes crashing. But in between waves, there is life.

Somewhere down the line, and it's different for everybody, you find that the waves are only 80 feet tall. Or 50 feet tall. And while they still come, they come further apart. You can see them coming. An anniversary, a birthday, or Christmas, or landing at O'Hare. You can see it coming, for the most part, and prepare yourself. And when it washes over you, you know that somehow you will, again, come out the other side. Soaking wet, sputtering, still hanging on to some tiny piece of the wreckage, but you'll come out.

Take it from an old guy. The waves never stop coming, and somehow you don't really want them to. But you learn that you'll survive them. And other waves will come. And you'll survive them too. If you're lucky, you'll have lots of scars from lots of loves. And lots of shipwrecks.

Reddit on-line forum community.
User : G/snow.

CHAPTER   4

When Grief Gets Messy

Grief is a complicated topic, and grief is... Messy!

I could not find a better word to describe grief. I looked up the definition of "messy" after choosing it as my single word descriptor. I found a list of other words including: chaotic, confused, disarray, bitter, unpleasant, awkward, complicated, complex, tricky, problematic, distressing and painful. That's a good start to describing grief. Moving through grief does not always go smoothly. It may complicate many areas of our lives and our ability to function.

Grief is like a garden. It needs to be tended, checked on, nourished, and nurtured. You cannot just plant a seed and expect that time alone will grow a healthy blooming plant. Unexpected pests and weeds may work their way into your beautiful garden and make it messy. If you don't attend to it daily, you will not know there are weeds and pests in your garden! Likewise, you need to know what to look for while you are grieving. If you think of your mind and emotions as a garden, you may find it is tangled with offshoots of grief. I will help you to identify those weeds so you know what to look for and how to "root" them out. As you rejuvenate your personal "garden," blooms will sprout.

What We Know for Sure

We know that grief can become very messy when ignored, just as a beautiful garden will become tangled and choked with weeds if it is not tended. We know how to clean up a messy garden, but how do we clean up messy grief? Let's consider what grievers have in common. There are a few things we know for sure that are characteristic of this universal experience. Let's continue to expand our understanding and tend to grief and loss.

Despite the fact that humans all grieve and share many similarities as they experience grief, **grieving makes most of us uncomfortable**. We don't know what to do with all the thoughts and feelings that show up. The list of feelings from the book introduction, or the synonyms for "messy" above, are a sampling of the feelings we may experience. This tangling of feelings may include confusion, numbness, anxiety, emptiness, anger, sadness, loneliness, guilt, relief, shock, depression and feeling overwhelmed. It may be difficult to manage all these feelings, and sort through thoughts, affecting our ability to make solid decisions, know how and when to react, or what is okay to express.

You may lack energy to manage and balance the depth of this personal experience while dealing with the outside world. While you are in turmoil, the rest of the world keeps turning. People get up, go to work, feed their kids, pay bills, and drop the car off at the shop. All this activity continues and may require your attention while your world seems to have stopped. The rest of the world continues to nurture their gardens, maybe not noticing that all attention to yours has stopped. This may leave you confused and isolated. You may feel that no one else could understand what you are going through. This may prompt you to isolate yourself or feel alone in your experience.

You may not want to "burden" others with your sadness and tears, making them uncomfortable. Even while affected by loss, we worry about what others think and we do not want to feel "needy." Grievers, and those around them, often expect that we should cruise through our grief at top speed to *get through it* so that others don't have to be uncomfortable.

Unless others have experienced the heaviness of loss, especially a traumatic loss, they might not have the knowledge to effectively support you. They don't know what to say to you as you grieve, even if it's a shared loss. Your support system can fall back on clichés' or even fall silent. Others may avoid you because of their discomfort. They want to say the right thing, but may say anything that comes to mind or nothing at all. Others may pretend nothing has happened, hoping not to remind you of your loss.

It often does not occur to people to just ask these straightforward questions: "What do you need? How can I help?" or to say, "What can I pick up for you at the store?" or "I'll pick up the kids from school." I encourage your loved ones to say: "I feel uncomfortable or inadequate to help at this moment; please help me to support you." Then the guessing game is over. With direct responses to those questions and statements, people can feel useful and relieve awkwardness by taking action. It can really be that simple!

Circumstances around the loss can be discomforting. If your loved one completed suicide, you may experience devastating pain, but you may feel reluctant sharing this detail, fearing the reactions of others. Such fears can complicate grief and separate us from the support of others. Isolation may be accompanied by feelings of guilt or helplessness and unanswered questions. Coping styles of others can throw us off balance. We all express our grief in different ways, some of us are boisterous and expressive, others quiet or withdrawn.

After I lost a close friend I was asked "How are you doing?" so many times that the question created its own awkwardness and stress! It either made my head spin, my frustration peak, or I wanted to cry. I told my friends "Please stop asking me!" I learned this is not the best question to ask. I have revised it to: "How are you making it today?"

That's a question people can hear, contemplate, and answer. It feels caring and supportive without suggesting there is something wrong with me:) So please take this advice, it will keep communication open and flowing.

Another common concern is "Am I grieving properly?" **There is no right or wrong way to experience your grief, as long as you are PRESENT and actually IN the experience.** Avoid shaping your grief by what others do and express, or even how you moved through the last loss that you encountered. Grief is not a logical event that can be scripted.

We are individuals with a wide variety of reactions to loss. We may be very emotional, calm, numb, or matter of fact about our losses. There's a wide range of "normal" thoughts, feelings and behaviors when grieving. There is plenty of room to experience grief. And please don't take cues from movies and television; that's just entertainment.

Perspectives on grieving shift and change based on our circumstances, relationships, past losses, and faith. Returning to the garden analogy, there are many "right" ways to plant and tend to your garden. Your garden's requirements will vary, just as your soil, crop, and sunlight vary, even from that of your closest neighbors. Pay close attention to what your unique grief/garden needs from you.

Consider the suddenness of the loss, the support we have, and the mental and emotional stability of ourselves and those around us. We experience loss as individuals. Aim for grieving in a "healthy way," not **the** right way. Avoid falling into the trap of "right or wrong," or worse, the need to grieve "perfectly," as there is no such thing.

Grief is emotionally exhausting and physical exhaustion is also part of grief. You may have no energy and feel you are dragging yourself around. It may be difficult to sleep or you may want to sleep all the time. Grief can bring a sense of heaviness in the body. Often people get this confused with feeling run-down, or coming down with a cold, but emotional pain can be very physically taxing. As I describe this to clients and patients, heads begin to nod with recognition and ah-ha's about, "So that was what was going on with me." It is important to take care of your physical body as well as your emotions while grieving.

If you delay or stuff your grief, it will wait for you. It simply will not just fade away. Like weeds in a garden, pretending you don't see them does not change their pesky presence. We can be emotionally overwhelmed, distracted, or numb at the time of a loss and not "get around" to experiencing and acknowledging our feelings. We may put them on the back burner while we deal with what seems more pressing at the time. If so, those feelings will sit in the back of your heart waiting for the next loss to show up in your life and then float to the surface waiting for its turn to be processed. This could happen weeks or even decades later, catching you by surprise. I have seen the look of recognition as someone puts these pieces together.

I have worked with clients with losses up to 50 years earlier. One mature woman said, "I want to grieve the loss of my Father.", She proudly stated her age and that it had been almost 60 years ago, but as a child she did not get the opportunity and did not know how to grieve. I had the privilege of witnessing the memories flood back and her tears of both sadness and joy.

Grief often underlies mental health problems, substance use and other difficult life issues. If there is a history of mental health issues such as depression or anxiety, or you struggle with substance abuse, grief is more likely to be unresolved. If life was already off balance, things may be exacerbated by this new crisis. You may already need to feel in control of what is happening in your life with family, work, or relationships when you encounter a loss. The desire may arise to numb, hide, minimize, or deny this overwhelming news. You may self-medicate to achieve this goal. The instability of your mood may become worse or substance use may spike to compensate for the need to be absent.

Remember, all these pieces factor into creating and maintaining the "garden." We need to be present to notice the weeds, even when they make us uncomfortable. We must speak up for what we need, accept help, and take the time for self-care to lessen fatigue and have energy to tend to the tangled thoughts and weeds. Lastly, know that you are the garden; fertilize it with hope, and allow your feelings to nurture it. Give it the care it needs to thrive and bloom once again.

The Dynamics of Grief

There are commonalities within the grieving experiences, but grief is also unique and messy, and we each need to attend to our own. The dynamics of grief create weeds in our garden; understanding these dynamics is another step toward addressing grief at its roots.

You may be reading this book because grief is new to you, or perhaps you already had an overwhelming loss in your life that you want to understand and feel ready now to sort through your feelings of grief. That was part of Jason's story. He conveyed the trouble he was having attaching to, and explaining his feelings to me. I told him this was normal. Grief exhibits many forms including complicated, chronic, or delayed. The concept of complicated grief may be unfamiliar to you. Let's discuss what creates complicated grief and how it relates to you as you grieve the loss of a loved one. Defining grief in this way may help you understand why it may be so difficult to feel and move through overwhelming loss.

Some examples of these characterizations of grief can help you understand how and why this affects you during the grieving process. Complicated, chronic and delayed grief are not exclusive. You may experience more than one of them at a time based on circumstances. Your grief may be complicated and chronic, complicated and delayed and in some situations complicated, chronic and delayed.

Let's start with understanding what these terms mean when you are grieving so you can compare it to your life event and begin to recognize how your path toward healing may be affected.

Complicated Grief

When Jason shared his story about the sudden loss of his Mother when he was a young child, and his Father's inability to show emotions and help him through the loss of his Mom, I heard so many factors that led Jason down some of the roads he traveled and influenced choices he made in life. I showed him how his inability to express some of his feelings not only related to his grief, but other areas of his life. Grief had influenced and directed parts of his life story.

A psychologist who specializes in grief and loss, defined complicated grief and developed a framework to help us understand the messy elements of our grief experience.

"An intense grief reaction, which leads to the person becoming overwhelmed, resorting to maladaptive behaviors or remaining in a state of grief which disallows progression of the mourning process to completion."

Basically, the definition says the intensity of grief may overwhelm us, leading us to turn away, avoid, or distract ourselves from those feelings by over-working, minimizing our experience and feelings, or using substances to numb out and escape feelings and challenges life presents after a loss.

I could see several of these elements at work in Jason's story. His youthful experience with grief was intense and confusing. He became distracted and avoided feelings as his father had done. Later in life, Jason continued to struggle with feeling deeply and found that alcohol helped him feel, express himself, numb out or unwind. You may feel a connection to Jason's story as you hear details of his loss and his reactions to it. If we are distracted, we are not progressing or moving through our grief. Some of us describe feeling stuck, directionless, overwhelmed, cried out, tearless, or numb. Grief is messy and complicated.

In my practice, the stated purpose of the initial visit does not always shine light on what the underlying factors or details may be. Complicated grief may be an unaddressed issue unconsciously causing havoc. Based on personal experiences, decades in this field professionally, and independent research, I've conceptualized various scenarios and situations that contribute to complicated grief. I routinely turn to these in my sessions and walk my patients through them, to help uncover the depth and root of their grief dynamics. I often see factors adding up to complicated, chronic or delayed grief. I created a list of situations contributing to complicated grief. Some of these may be relevant to your loss. This is not an all-inclusive list as your pain, your love, and the life you have shared with your loved one cannot be packaged. In some instances, it only takes one element to cause grief to be complicated, although you may relate to a large number of the possible complicating situations. This may help you understand the pain you are experiencing, the amount of time that it might take to move through your grief toward peace, and why the feelings may seem at times overpowering. Grief may currently be in the driver's seat in your life.

> *"Every day is a puzzle,*
> *you may feel*
> *differently every day"*
>
> ~ GV

Complicated grief may result when any situations like the following occur:

Sudden or Unanticipated Loss

Victoria was only ten years old when the unthinkable happened. She was playing in her room with her sister when she looked out back and saw her Mother lying on the lawn. It was clear she was not lounging or resting, she was not moving. Victoria and her seven-year-old sister Ashley ran from the house to the backyard. They hovered over their Mother calling her name. She was barely responsive. So, while Ashley stayed with her, Victoria ran to the neighbor's house seeking help. There was no answer. She returned home and called 911, but by the time help arrived, her Mother had passed away and there was nothing to be done. Victoria lived with the idea of not being able to save her Mother for over 25 years and that's when I met her.

When the unthinkable happens and catches you off guard, it is hard to wrap your head around what you are experiencing. Life-changing events often happen on typical days, as you go about managing your home, family needs, and job responsibilities. Then the phone rings or someone knocks on the door and your world is never the same again. This type of loss may happen at the least likely time and to the least likely person you can imagine. Perhaps it is a young person who was in fine health. It may be someone mature who is feisty and full of energy. Either way, we did not see it coming. It may be a tragic accident, an act of nature or some peculiar circumstances.

Because you cannot anticipate such a tragedy, there is no time to brace yourself, or ground yourself to prepare for the news emotionally and mentally. It throws us off balance and we may feel our world has been turned upside down. Shock and denial can make you feel numb and disoriented. Difficulty getting beyond shock and denial under these circumstances is common.

For Victoria, it left her on high alert, and fearful of changes in her life. She became angry and controlling in her significant relationships, not connecting her behavior to the need to be in control that was driven by the sudden loss she experienced. This long-term impact makes her grief complicated.

Most of us like to be in charge and in control of all circumstances, not only in our lives, but in our loved ones lives as well. Lack of control may lead to feeling helpless. You may not be able to figure out where to begin, what to do, how to proceed. Sudden tragedy may make it impossible for you to be there at the time of a loved one's need, or present for their last breath. If there is a distance to travel it may be unrealistic to be present "in time."

You may not be within your support circle to receive support from other loved ones. Humans are built to connect, and it is these connections that allow us to share the depth of our sorrow and receive and give comfort. This goes a long way toward healing. Sudden loss may make it impossible to be present or attend a service or celebration of life, which may lead to other complicated feelings or a lack of closure. Victoria learned how her complicated grief triggered behaviors of keeping people at a distance, and needing to be in control. Once understood, she was able to take more risks, allow people to get closer, and share control which strengthened her relationships.

Death Following a Long Illness

Trent's father, James was diagnosed with lung cancer while Trent was away at college. James assured him that he would be okay and that Trent should move on with the education they both wanted for his life. Trent was an aspiring engineer with big dreams. Unfortunately, when he came home for the holidays, his Father had seriously deteriorated. He was a shadow of the man Trent had last seen. James was straight-forward, and told him that although he was fighting this, it did not look like he would survive. Trent spent every bit of spare time he could coming home to be with his Dad over the next year, but was still caught off-guard when his father died the next summer.

You might think that a loved one passing away after a long illness would be easier to comprehend. A long illness may prepare us in some ways for what is coming. We have heard the diagnosis, been to the doctor's appointments, and held our loved one's hand through chemotherapy. You may have been the primary caregiver, helping them day in and day out with the task of maintaining health. Your presence may have helped them hold on a bit longer, or made your loved one as comfortable and pain free as possible. It can be years from the message of a diagnosis, the health battle, the fight to survive, and the loss of life. However, this knowledge may have little impact on the intensity of our feelings when that moment of death actually arrives. While our loved ones are still here with us, anticipation can aid us in beginning the grief process.

I believe that we grieve twice. We begin grieving when we learn the bad news of a diagnosis and we are touched by feelings of grief. As we look at the stages of grief, we may feel like we are already moving through them, naturally or with reluctance. It may start with *disbelief* of the diagnosis, and *sadness* as we think of what this means for our loved one. We want to *deny* that this is happening, get a second opinion, and run the test again. We become *angry* that they, and we ourselves, have to go through this painful experience. We may be saddled late into the night with thoughts buzzing, "*what if' and I wish.*" At some point you may feel you have *accepted* this reality for your loved one and yourself, acceptance of what is to come and knowledge that it's just a matter of time, only to find yourself navigating through the above feelings and thoughts, along with many others, again and again.

No one wants to watch someone they love slowly deteriorate, or suffer physical or emotional pain, and become a shadow of themselves. These circumstances lead to even more agony as you grieve for the person while they are still here. You visit in the hospital, hospice, or home, witness their suffering and their surrender to the knowledge that life is coming to an end. An end of suffering may be welcomed by your loved one and you are not the only one thinking this way. You are not a horrible person. These feelings are normal. Sometimes it is just reality.

These thoughts may lead to guilt for feeling relieved the person is gone. This is hard for loved ones to voice, as it makes them feel even more guilty and/or selfish for even thinking these words, let alone verbalizing them. Give yourself permission to have this relief, as it is usually wished for only because the loved one's suffering is over.

The surprise is that when our loved one actually passes away, we may still feel stunned, unprepared, and not ready for it. I have heard many family members say, "Of course I knew this was going to happen... but, I just did not think it was going to be today." Feelings of grief may start fresh and we may loop back into our shock and denial. It is the finality, the reality that we just cannot anticipate. We cannot truly begin this phase of grieving until we have experienced this finality.

For Trent, not being able to spend more time with his father left him with guilt and regret and made his grief complicated. He began to second guess his decisions, allowing for every possible scenario...just in case. He was stuck. I helped Trent focus on what he gave his father, and the trust and richness of their relationship, with less focus on the times Tom could not be there. This promoted healing and peace.

Loss of a Child

Rachel was in her early twenties when she moved back home with her 6-year-old daughter Bethany, following the break-up of her marriage. Rachel was at a point in her life where she was figuring out her next moves and happy to have the support of her family. Rachel enjoyed just being a Mom and having this time to watch her daughter grow. They enjoyed the routine of playing, making picnic lunches together, and reading in the evenings. One day Rachel took a phone call as Bethany sat curiously beside her. Bethany grew bored and told her Mom she was going to get one of her dolls. Shortly after, when Rachel was off the phone she called for her daughter, who did not answer. She searched for her as they loved to play hide and seek. Rachel checked all her favorite places to no avail and began to feel panic arise as she thought, " She left the house!"

She raced to the yard to find her daughter had been hit by a car. The traumatic loss of her daughter started years of self-destructive behaviors, starting with numbing with alcohol, moving to relationships with abusive men, and on to binge eating to fill the emptiness she experienced for years. This is when I met Rachel, as she was seeking help for her poor self-care and relationship with food.

It is an unwritten rule that no parent should outlive his or her child. Loss of a child leads to thoughts of unfairness and questions of faith. It can shake your foundation and your relationship with a spouse or partner. Unfairness is a common theme around loss of a child. Someone so young is gone at a tender, innocent age, before they even begin to bloom. Thoughts of unfairness are closely trailed by the one word that keeps reverberating through your mind: "Why?" So many "why's" that keep us contemplating and renegotiating this incredibly painful loss. A secondary loss relates to the innocence a child carries, and the potential for years of life ahead that are now gone. We anguish over all the future plans that have ceased to have meaning.

The pain of the loss of a child is unbearable. I will never pretend to understand how that feels. Parents feel alone because no one else can possibly understand what this is like for them. This loneliness can tear at your heart and may isolate you from others, even your own partner. There may be a sense of responsibility and guilt, even when logically you know it is not your fault, that "it was an accident." All these factors make grief complicated. During the height of grief, this may be hard to understand. It is too logical a message when you are immersed in the emotional. An intuitive sense of responsibility stifles logic and comfort. Yet, the reality of parenting is that it is impossible to cocoon a child in a safe place 24 hours a day. A parent can spend a full day determined not to let a child fall, rushing behind them diligently trying to catch them every time they stumble. But even with this amount of attention and determination, the child will eventually fall.

The loss of a child may cause strife or separation of parents. Although some studies show a high rate of relationship discord, recent studies found that over 70% of parental relationships survive the loss of a child. Parents analyze the event and circumstances, negotiate what they should have done differently, where they should have been, what they said or didn't say, and often blame each other in the blur of the blinding pain. Reaching out for help from support groups specific to parents who have lost a child can be helpful and healing. Most communities have such resources for in-person meetings or even on-line groups or chatting. Rachel was able to be present with her grief for the first time in years. This allowed the healing of her heart, along with the end to years of self-destructive punishing behaviors.

A Troubled Pre-morbid Relationship

My relationship with my mother can definitely be described as troubled and complicated. We struggled with our connection and communication for as long as I can remember. This caused me to be distant and protective of my feelings.

Our relationship remained superficial until the end of her life. As a teen, it left me longing for a mother figure, which I sought and received from the moms of my friends. At times I felt uncertain and learned to be very cautious as I entered any kind of relationship. I understood the risk.

If you were struggling with your relationship with your loved one before their passing, whether a long-term feud or a recent spat of unpleasant words, it creates conflict in your mind and heart. We may have mixed feelings about the passing, including guilt about what we did or said, and bad feelings about how we behaved. We may experience relief as the constant turmoil and anxiety of trying to walk on eggshells, or choosing words carefully to avoid offending, is no longer necessary. Such feelings make the griever feel very uncomfortable. These thoughts and feelings often go unshared due to fear that others will not understand, further complicating our grief. We may wish it had been the perfect relationship, or even grieve not having had the kind of relationship we wanted with our parent, sibling, partner, or friend. A tendency to isolate may feel like the best or the only solution, if we are uncomfortable sharing.

You may be feeling things were unfinished, with a sense of no closure. Your loved one may have left this world with the last words between you being angry ones, with no time to correct and mend hard feelings or misunderstandings. Tumultuous relationships can create this lack of closure; words that didn't get shared, or experiences that caused strife in the relationship can no longer be resolved. You may become crowded with challenging feelings and thoughts of negotiating a better version of the relationship by minimizing behaviors and rethinking events. You can get stuck on "what ifs" that would bring closure. These final contacts may also cause guilt and resentment, depending on the details of your story. These situations may leave you confused about how you feel about the loss. There are ways to move toward acceptance in strained relationships. Even after your loved one has gone, there are still opportunities and avenues to find some peace within yourself without the presence of your loved one. For me, I learned to practice what I preach. This got me beyond the complications of my grief. Some ways to begin healing from these heavy feelings are discussed in Section Two of this book. This may also be a time where professional help can be very effective.

Multiple Losses

The loss you are currently experiencing may be the latest of a string of ungrieved losses. Several scenarios can make it difficult or impossible to grieve. I will never forget my new client Kevin, when I went out to greet him, he was wearing sunglasses. Hmm, I wondered what that was about. Maybe a migraine, maybe he had been crying? Maybe he just loved those glasses. Who's to say, but I guess I would find out. There is a question on the first page of the new client paperwork, "Why are you here today?" He left it blank. Another mystery. As we began to talk, Kevin was not forthcoming about why he was there and I finally asked him," Would you like to tell me why you are here?" He began to tear up and responded with a heavy sigh, "This is so embarrassing; I can't believe I came to counseling for this." I responded, "Whatever it is, it's okay." The words finally left his mouth "my cat died" as he began to cry harder.

In empathy I responded, "Pets are important and they are family members too," thinking I would help him not minimize his loss. Through his tears he stated, "But you don't understand, I hated that cat; I only got this cat a month ago and it was tearing up everything in my house!" Then it was clear to me that this was not about the cat. As I pulled the string to the past, I found this young man had lost eight important people in his life over the previous three years. This was not about the cat; it was about all the grief and loss he had suffered, one loss after another. All this grief had remained undealt with. The cat was just the final straw that pushed him over the edge emotionally.

Inability to be present emotionally or physically causes complications. When you are bombarded by one loss after another, it is hard to determine where your attention should be directed. Do I feel about my father or deal with the more recent loss of my best friend? Do I deal with the loneliness of an empty nest or do I worry about the spouse who has broken my heart? It may not be realistic to attend to more than one misfortune at a time even when healthy and in our best state of mind. It takes a lot of energy, and energy is limited, so attentiveness to a loss may cause a struggle.

Multiple losses can be overwhelming and this correlation may only be subconsciously in our awareness. You might think previous losses would give you some predictability when the next loss comes along. However, it does not mean you know how you will react the next time a loss occurs. Things shift with each experience. We may feel as if there is a timestamp or a window of opportunity to grieve, coming with an expiration date. We can think the time has passed and give up on grieving or decide it is no longer necessary, but you may find the feelings persist. This was clearly the issue for Kevin. I am glad he found his way to discovering what the real issue was and began to address his grief. Just so you know, he did get another cat.

Stuffing your feelings and your grief may feel like the best or even the only option. If you have a tendency to stuff your feelings, one loss can be stacked on top of another and then another. I regard the body as a container and it can only hold so much before it begins to break down. Like a dam holding water, the more we stuff our feelings and experiences the greater the pressure. There must be a release valve or the damn breaks and overflows. Grief always finds a way to the surface, sometimes in very sneaky ways that you may not connect to grief, such as having difficulty getting out of the house, avoiding people, or pretending all is well while you carry on "normal" life. Or maybe it's a cat tearing up your couch. Countless distractions, self-made and otherwise, can point us toward stuffing our grief. The rest of our world continues to move along at its usual pace as we attempt to balance grieving and our other responsibilities.

> *"Losses from the past*
> *may fuel the*
> *present painful fire"*
>
> ~ GV

Violent Death

Carrying a similar intensity to sudden death, violent death holds an extra burden. Violent death can be the result of a freak accident, a loved one's death by suicide, or other painful endings to life. You may be left with paralyzing thoughts of your loved one experiencing pain or suffering, even if you were not present when the incident occurred. Freak accidents are on the news every day. These unexpected odd circumstances are unpredictable and may leave you asking "How could this happen?" We can become hypervigilant and startle easily after these losses. There may be fears that your loved one was suffering or in a lot of pain because of the violent ending to their life. There may be a drive to get answers and learn details, taking over your time and attention as you forget about the other necessities that must be dealt with in life.

Violent death may cause great sadness yet a sense of relief that your loved one did not feel any pain or discomfort at the end. When a loved one's life is taken by another person, you feel helpless, and an intense anger might build and be directed into energy to right a wrong, seek justice, or change laws. Anger related to wrongful death can also be internalized and eat at you, gnaw at your soul, and make it difficult to move through grief or even function in daily life. These circumstances and feelings interfere with your base sense of loss and can distract you from your grieving. This makes grief complicated. Sadly, suicide has by far surpassed deaths from disease or motor vehicle accidents in this country. Every day people lose the battle with depression, addiction and hopelessness, deciding the only solution to their pain is to depart life.

Unfortunately for loved ones, losing someone to suicide comes with many emotional complications. Those left behind struggling with all the "normal" feelings of loss bear an additional burden when someone takes their own life. Family and friends may not want to share this information out of guilt, a sense of responsibility, or not trusting others' reactions to your loved one losing their battle with depression, addiction or overwhelming emotions. We can get isolated, creating a bubble of secrecy that prevents us from fully being in our feelings. For grievers, bargaining and being trapped in "What if's?" is common. You may replay the last time you saw your loved one or that last conversation over and over again, looking for hints and clues you may have missed. Sometimes, there are none. Reaching out to a support group specific to those who have lost loved ones to suicide can be extremely helpful.

We must do more for family members and friends suffering with mental illness and addiction. Each of us can help remove the stigma that comes with it. I believe in "mental hygiene." I pine for a day when our loved ones feel comfortable asking for help and have the resources they need to help them through times of helplessness and hopelessness. This is not an end all solution, but would make a difference. Suicide is more prevalent than we wish to think. Just one example is the statistic for our military heroes with staggering loss of life by suicide: 22 souls each day.

For Evelyn, the thought of her daughter Regina intentionally running her car into a tree was unbearable. Evelyn began having visions of Regina being crushed in her car and this led to sleepless nights. If sleep came, nightmares followed. She carried guilt and the despair of not having been aware of her daughter's desperate thoughts. She over-analyzed their last conversations, looking for what she might have missed. All this turmoil made her grief very complicated. Images of violent death can remain in your head, or follow you in your dreams. Even if we were not present at the scene, our minds can imagine what it must have been like and will create images to fill in the blanks that haunt us. I have consulted with clients suffering from post-traumatic stress disorder (PTSD) who did not witness the traumatic events, but were affected through their disturbing imaginings.

Evelyn was able to find peace in the reassurances of her support system and embrace the self-forgiveness she had felt impossible months earlier. This took time, therapy, and faith.

Perceived Issues of Preventability or Randomness

Loss that is random or perceived as having been preventable may initiate dozens of scenarios through your head, focusing on how, why, the timing, and the ways this random, preventable loss might have turned out as a benign near miss. This type of loss, including suicide, may create an atmosphere where you get stuck in bargaining and wanting things to be different. You may struggle to make sense of what happened and become overwhelmed with the question of "Why?" Sleepless nights and inability to clear your mind are common.

Frustration can build as you try to make sense of something that is senseless. Questions and negotiating different outcomes become a priority over life's daily routine and responsibilities. This may spiral into feelings of loss of control, and even put you on high alert for random events. For Cory, walking in on the robbery of her home changed her life. As her husband Jacob protected her, he was shot. After his death, she felt helpless. She said she had not slept through the night for over a year. Cory ran the scenario over and over, each time changing an element: the time they arrived home, if they had stopped at the store as they originally planned they would not have been there and so forth. Cory fears that something else tragic could or might happen, making her extra cautious of her surroundings, people, cars, or any sign of illness.

After a perceived preventable tragedy, you may become hypervigilant. This high level of alertness steals much needed energy from other parts of your life. Another consequence of preventable or random loss is a tendency to grasp for control in other areas of your life to feel more grounded. Unpredictability is a sensitive spot for most of us as we fight for control in uncontrollable situations. Seeking control may be the strongest pull within you, because being in control comforts us. It is human nature to look for ways to stabilize yourself by steadying your mind, body, family, support systems, and grounding in beliefs and faith. In other words, you want to stop the boat from rocking and get anchored. Cory found her way by focusing on situations she could control and, more importantly, getting back to grieving the loss of her husband instead of staying in the mind trap of continuing to try to renegotiate the outcome of her husband's death.

Mental Health or Substance abuse Prior to Loss

Suffering and death of a loved one due to mental health issues or substance use can leave us with lots of questions and heavy hearts. As a friend or family member you may have been involved with years of the up and down spirals of your loved one as they lived with depression, anxieties, or continued relapses on alcohol and drugs. These experiences can be debilitating for all involved. You may have pushed them into a doctor's office for medications, or encouraged them to seek outpatient or inpatient treatment. These attempts may have failed, leaving you with feelings of frustration, helplessness, and fear for your loved one.

As grievers, we can get stuck in the thoughts that we "should" have done more, known more, or pushed harder. This can lead to restless nights and the heavy feelings of responsibility, even when it is unreasonable to blame yourself. We may not ask for the support we need out of fear of others not understanding or wanting to avoid talking about the struggles of your lost love.

When Harris lost his sister Maddie to her long battle with depression and alcohol abuse, he came to see me about the guilt he carried. He repeatedly said he "should" have known this was going to happen, and stopped it. Many circumstances in our lives we would like to "do over" because they leave us in emotional pain. But we don't have the kind of superpowers it would take to be all knowing and control the life of another. Once Harris understood this, he could begin to let go of this guilty feeling that weighed him down and kept him stuck in his grief.

Lack of Closure

Lack of closure results from a variety of events or situations. Many areas of complicated grief discussed above may lead to this additional challenge. You may think a distant relationship should be easier to move through when you are grieving, but the same unfinished business, the discussions that did not happen or the unresolved conflicts, make it messy. Now the opportunity to repair the relationship has passed and will not return. This can leave you with feelings of guilt, resentment, or anger.

Anger is an interesting feeling; we gravitate toward it. As we search for control, anger feels powerful. If abandonment defined your relationship, closure might not occur. Abandonment usually has taken a toll and shaped the relationship. You may be feeling the loss of closeness and grieve the lack of connection with someone you wanted to be important in your life. Now you grieve a second time, as they are no longer here and you embrace the finality of the relationship.

Another avenue to lack of closure is not being present at the time of death. I have witnessed loved ones carry much regret for not being there in those final moments. Often it is unpreventable: you could not get there fast enough. Sometimes other events or crises do not allow us to be there and hold the hand of a loved one as they slip away. This complication can leave a sense of longing to re-negotiating a different ending. It may seem there is nowhere to place those last words, prayers, or reassurances of love we have for the person. This leaves the griever feeling off balance and with no way to repair the issues.

If the relationship was troubled, sometimes it is unclear just what we are grieving. Is it the relationship we had or the one we wished we could have had? Frequently, missed opportunities for a healthy connected relationship leaves us with longing and frustration that we did not have enough time. Second-guessing yourself and decisions you have made about the relationship (including boundaries you may have set) may become a focus in your mind. With your loved one gone, it is impossible to fix or shift the relationship. Hope is a powerful feeling and when it is doused you may feel empty or helpless.

Lack of closure can be caused by not being able to be there when your loved one takes their last breath or being unable to attend services or a celebration of life. Frequently people are grounded in the finality of death by these events.

Not being present in that critical final moment may not be up to you. Sometimes patients do not want to be witnessed as they slip away. I have seen patients wait until a family member leaves the bedside to take a much-needed break to get a cup of coffee, stretch their legs, or make a phone call. The patient slips away when there is no one to witness those final moments. The will of the patient can be strong and family members may not have heard of this kind of strong-willed departure. Families may feel guilty for leaving the room or thinking of themselves for a few minutes.

I have seen the opposite, where patients hold on until their loved ones fly across the country to be present before they pass away, wanting to hear their voice or feel their touch one last time. Who can say why the end of life plays out as it does? I believe we have to gently guide ourselves toward acceptance.

Lack of closure is intertwined with factors of complicated grief. It can be a puzzle because no closure occurs when our loss is sudden, unpredictable, or random. Inability to be emotionally present due to your mental or emotional health, or if your energy is focused on another loss, can make closure seem distant. You may get lost in the hypervigilance of trauma, a tumultuous relationship, images of your loved one in pain, or the multiple questions all beginning with the word "Why?" We cannot understand the suddenness or that the long- anticipated moment of loss finally arrived. If we are stuck in feelings of guilt and resentment, and lack the support we need to voice our struggles, it may be a much longer and complicated journey toward healing.

Chronic Grief

While many people experience loss without needing assistance, chronic grief may indicate a need to seek support. Inability to move through your grief, or a sense of being stuck, sometimes years after your loss, suggests chronic grief. Many circumstances contribute to chronic grief. My client Jeanette came to see me for the on-going emotional distress experienced after her co-worker and friend Brenda passed away. Brenda and Jeanette had worked as a team troubleshooting corporate issues, and were labeled "the dynamic duo" by their peers. After Brenda died, Jeanette was lost. Her grief was continually triggered each day as she sat at her desk with Brenda not there. Two years after her loss, Jeanette sought advice about inability to focus and be productive. She considered leaving her job because she could no longer tolerate this pain. Her situation is a good example of chronic grief defined as:

"An *on-going*, prolonged experience with *no significant* reduction in emotional distress. Experienced *pain* and *sadness* that is *triggered* by *events*. The inability to move through the grief process due to *on-going circumstances* such as chronic *life issues* or *health conditions*."

Chronic Grief Can be Triggered by a Variety of Circumstances

Those who were in a close relationship with a loved one, with their loved one an intricate part of daily routine and functioning, must forge a new way. This can leave you struggling with grief for longer periods. The home you shared, pictures, music, the TV show you watched together every Thursday night, all can trigger grief. Jeannette could now see how daily reminders of Brenda affected her inability to move through her grief. Once she identified these triggers, she could allow herself to feel the emotions of her loss, and then find a way to honor her partnership with Brenda by completing a special project at work.

An enmeshed relationship (where you made few decisions without the concurrence of your loved one) may leave you with a lack of direction or purpose. Feeling lost can make grief linger. Your loved one may have been entwined in your community, with well-wishers paying on-going respect. Grief may be continually triggered by reminders of a tragedy. Driving down a street where the accident occurred, or seeing someone who was spared, triggers memories of your loved one.

Chronic life challenges, such as relationships requiring your time and energy, turn you away from grieving and may prolong your grief. Career demands that increase as your patient employer awaits your return and full attention to your work, can disrupt the grief process. You may have physical and emotional challenges testing your ability to be present with your grief without becoming overwhelmed. Depression and anxiety might take top priority, and be a chronic reminder of your loss. As these feelings deepen, they may prevent you from noticing your grief is still there awaiting your awareness and attention. Managing chronic physical health issues may require focus to stay in adequate health. If you must worry about your blood sugar levels, medication regimen, or physical therapy, grief may once again need to wait.

Continual use or dependency on alcohol or drugs can keep you vacillating between numbing out your thoughts and feelings and being overcome by them. One of my clients, Stephen, reported all his feelings resurfaced after he became sober. He had struggled with his addiction off and on for the last 5 years and noted his use increased after he lost his mentor, Tyler. Stephen was used to turning to alcohol to avoid his feelings and challenges. When Tyler died, it was easy for Stephen to rationalize his use and dependency. I have met so many people like him with feelings waiting to be explored when they return to full consciousness. When Tyler died, Stephen was so bent on not being emotionally present that not only did he break his sobriety, he took two part time jobs in addition to his full-time job. He worked seven days a week for almost a year, leaving no time for grieving. Yet there it was, along with his sobriety, awaiting his attention 5 years later. All these scenarios cause a sense of persistent grief, like an undercurrent continually moving in the background of our lives.

Once Stephen was able to identify the motivations for his behaviors and directly address his grief and feelings, he was able to open up emotionally about other issues in his life and refocused his attention on his recovery.

Delayed Grief

Busy lifestyles may delay our experience of grief. In our society, we are pulled in many directions. We have layers of responsibility for family, career, and ourselves. This can swallow the physical and emotional time needed to sit with our grief. Delayed grief defined simply means we were unable to experience our feelings of loss at the time the loss occurred.

Our way of life, daily pressures, and expectations promote delayed grief. As we begin to grieve, we watch life's demands and our career responsibilities stack up, awaiting our returned attention. Standard bereavement leave is three days, which only allows time to begin the process of grieving. After a significant loss it will take months, sometimes longer, for us to regain our bearings. Yet there are real or self-imposed expectations to return to work and act "normal" while carrying our unresolved pain of loss. Under these circumstances, grief may seep out over months or years, trying to find the path of healing. It may show up as an inability to concentrate and focus on tasks, memory lapses, fatigue, or seeming emotionlessness to the outside world as you try to "hold it together." Grief needs time to be your priority.

Circumstances of the loss, be it a tumultuous relationship, other losses around that time, or inability to be present due to our own health problems or distractors, can all delay the start of our route through grief. If you are a "stuffer," someone who takes feelings and minimizes them or tucks them away with the real or imagined intent that "I will get back to that," you might harbor grief that awaits your returned attention. These delays have consequences. Anxiety specific to death or other life issues may increase, or depression may overtake you. You may distance yourself from others, or feel unease in general. These emotions, moods and ways of relating to others can be your body's attempt to tell you to slow down and grieve.

I see clients who have harbored the pain of loss for years without slowing down to attend to their pain or need to grieve. It is never too late to grieve. Here are a few specific situations that can be at the root of delayed grief:

Timing

Time is a challenge for most of us as we navigate through life's demands. If you have multiple traumatic or intense issues at once, what gets the attention? Now and then, circumstances in life align such that we can neither be physically or emotionally present at the same time.

This was the position Ursula found herself in. Ursula had met a charming gentleman when he traveled on business from the USA to her home country. They fell in love and married. She moved away from her home and close-knit family and began a new life in the USA. As she began to learn the language and settle into a new country, home, and lifestyle, she discovered she was pregnant. When she called home to share the news, she also learned some sad news. Her sister Greta had a terminal diagnosis. This put Ursula over the edge. She had maneuvered through so much change, and now she was anticipating losing her best friend, her sister. This knowledge caused uncertainty about her new life, an increased longing for home, and guilt about not being able to be present for her sister. The timing could not have been worse.

Timing is often beyond our control. Ursula, once aware her grief had been delayed over these last two years, she was able to prioritize her feelings and express her grief for Greta. She found balance and learned to express her needs for support from her family, near and abroad.

Age

Children don't possess the experience, understanding, and coping skills that seasoned adults have to manage grief. A child looks to parents, or an adult figure to see how this is done. If the adult is unable to be present and share thoughts and feelings, the child is unlikely to as well.

I introduced Jason to you earlier. His grief was delayed. He was 11 years old when he lost his mother to cancer. Unfortunately, his father shut down emotionally and Jason followed the only example he had by doing the same. This affected the way Jason dealt with other difficult situations and losses over the years. Shutting down, his "go to" for managing emotions, kept him isolated. Forty years later, Jason unearthed his feelings and sense of loss to grieve and heal. Jason repaired relationships with his family without the fear of abandonment.

Depending on a child's age, they may move through grief more easily. Preschool children do not understand that death is permanent. Children may struggle with magical thinking, that the parent can come back, or that something they did caused the parent to die. Keep communications open. Children ask questions when they are able to ask. No matter our age, we ask more questions when we are ready to hear the answers.

Pre-teens and teenagers, with more experience than younger children, recognize death as permanent. Teens begin to see and need a parent in a different way. There is an intense need for guidance and parental support, but connection shifts in teens as they spend more time outside of their immediate family, and friends and classmates become more important and formative in their lives. These circumstances and distractions can leave grief delayed.

As for younger children, under age 4, losing a parent creates a yearning for attachment. The child may be fussy, and need more routine and structure in their lives. Regardless of age, children may be confused, anxious, irritated, frightened, and need extra adult attention. They need to talk to and explore feelings with supportive adults where they feel accepted and heard.

Many adults with unresolved, delayed, childhood grief need to know it is never too late to grieve. The impression this loss has left on your life is worth exploring as it may affect how you connect in your relationships today. I discourage minimizing long-ago losses. Whether the loss was five or forty years ago, exploration can deepen your understanding of self and provide peace.

Emotional Instability

Life's challenges, or pre-existing emotional issues such as depression and anxiety, can leave us unequipped to manage a loss. We may have more than we can handle and no capacity to take on this new emotional strain. Delaying may seem a natural choice to avoid feeling overwhelmed. Those of us with depression may become more depressed and require additional emotional support, by seeking counseling or seeing your physician about medication. Anxiety symptoms may increase. New worries and fears may arise, including fear of death of self or other loved ones. A relatively predictable life helps decrease depression and anxious feelings. While emotions run high, there is little room for being present with grief.

Unfortunately, the following story is not rare. I received a referral from another therapist who was working with Daniel, a middle-aged man who came seeking help for depression. The therapist recognized a likelihood of alcohol dependency and sent him to see me for assessment. Daniel had a problem with alcohol and depression. He was self-medicating his complicated unresolved grief.

Daniel had lost his son Teddy 10 years earlier and had more recent losses. His teenage Godchild, Samantha, died in a tragic accident and Daniel's wife had recently lost a baby to miscarriage. Alcohol was a tool to numb out, not feel, and escape all these losses and the feelings that came with them. The irony is that while we are distracted by self-destructive behaviors like alcohol and substance use, grief can become chronic and/or delayed, waiting indefinitely for its turn to be felt. Daniel did not see that alcohol exacerbated his problems. He felt isolated, and this made him less able to cope emotionally. Once Daniel stopped drinking, he could deal with his underlying depression and use medication support to help him be available to grieve.

Fear of Loss of Control

Do you need life to be predictable? Those who need to be in charge have a hard time with situations they cannot control. We may fear feelings that would arise if we were truly present to experience loss. Fear of loss of control can be a reason to avoid or stuff grief. Some worry that if they begin to *really* feel feelings related to the loss, they might never recover, lose total control of their emotions, and shatter their predictable world. One client said, "If I start to cry, I may never stop!" This fear can cause us to dam up our feelings, not wanting to risk the possible fallout that could occur.

My client Oscar assumed the "No way, lady" posture, when I attempted to get him to be in touch with feelings on a deeper level. It took some time to build trust and a safe place for Oscar to talk about the feelings he had pushed away for decades. His fear had prevented the very thing he wanted in life, connection. Once he was feeling and witnessed that the dam had not burst, he began to heal old wounds, grieve, and have deeper, more meaningful relationships.

Family Roles and Responsibility

If you designated yourself, or have been designated by others in your support system, as the "Responsible person," there may be no time for you to grieve. The responsible person has to consider what needs to be done, and take care of getting it done. This includes healthcare decisions, caring for family members, and keeping all the moving pieces functioning. This role leaves little room for high emotions that disrupt responsibilities.

Caretaking can also distract you from your path through grief. This may be intentional or coincidence, leaving you feeling detached and distracted. Responsibilities can leave you craving time for yourself, to be in touch with feelings, and even resentful of being in this role. This can complicate and delay your grief. Family and support system roles are discussed further in Chapter 6.

Substance Use or Active Addiction

Addiction has many trials. A substance abuse crisis is on-going in the world. The number of people lost in the throes of addiction remains high. Unfortunately, only 10% of those with alcohol or drug dependency get the help they need to begin and maintain their recovery. Those in recovery or reaching for recovery have difficulty balancing life and emotions while learning and maintaining coping skills. Those experiencing loss during active addiction may be unable to be present, or intentionally use substances to be numb or absent and avoid feeling. Those new to recovery may relapse after loss. There is little progress with grief until we are fully present with our loss.

Addicts and "normies" alike sometimes find alcohol or substances enhances their ability to feel, be emotional, and share thoughts and feelings with others. This "liquid courage" can become an attractive, but dangerous option. Relying on substances to induce numbness or create emotions sets us up for further complications to grieving and managing emotional situations arising in life. This coping style can become a trap preventing you from addressing grief effectively, and leaving grief unresolved, chronic and delayed for years.

Previous Loss

If you had a previous loss, especially recently, it may be difficult to manage your feelings. You may be in the midst of exploring your grief about one loss when another comes along. In these instances, you may choose to push your past loss aside for the immediate crisis in front of you. You may choose not to deal with either, feeling overwhelmed and delaying for a *better time* to grieve, which may never come. Emotional trauma builds and is stored, ever waiting for you to explore it. The more you set grief aside, the fuller your unconscious emotional container becomes.

These are a few of the challenges making grief such a significant and emotional journey in life. You may have seen the overlaps in your own story, related to areas where you became stuck or overwhelmed. You may now find that the dynamics of your grief are more defined, or even messier. These dynamics can exist simultaneously and be interwoven. Your grief may not just be complicated, but also chronic or delayed. These situations and feelings leave grief unresolved.

As you learned from the descriptions of complicated, chronic and delayed grief, there can be many commonalities. Bobby's story shows how complicated, chronic and delayed grief may overlap.

Bobby was a cocaine addict in his mid 40's, one of the worst addictions I had seen. He had had two reconstructive surgeries to repair his nose from the damage of drug use. When he arrived voluntarily wanting treatment for his addiction, he was separated from his wife who "had enough." Bobby dug in and dug deep and did quite well with his sobriety. Three months into his treatment, he came in and told me "Good news! My wife and I are talking and I am hopeful we can get back together!"

Things progressed over the next few weeks and she returned home. Life was good, and they both worked hard at their relationship. Unfortunately, one month later, she was in a freak accident and passed away. Bobby was devastated and, not surprisingly, relapsed to using drugs. The accident was a hit and run and the driver was arrested within a week. Bobby felt he needed to be in the courtroom each day to represent his wife. That was extremely painful and kept him stuck in his grief and addiction. There is no way to move through grief when you are being re-traumatized daily.

Bobby's grief shows the dynamics and complicated factors I've listed. In fact, almost all fit Bobby's situation. His grief was chronic. He could not move through it as long as the trial was going on and it did not conclude for over 6 months. His grief was also delayed as he awaited the end of the trial to return to his path in recovery and be present with his emotions after this tragic loss.

It is important to identify the dynamics of your grief, allowing awareness to move you toward the "how" of healing. Once aware, there can be solutions! I have created the worksheet below to help you identify the details of your complicated journey through grief. This will create another piece of foundation in Section One, so we can move to solutions in Section Two, *The Five Written Expressions of Grief*™ or the *5WE's*.

Is My Grief Complicated?

As you reference each of these dynamics, notice how each complication adds to the bigger picture and how the intensity of your experience becomes more clear. This worksheet will help you look at the broad scope of your grief.

Complicated Grief

An **intense** grief reaction, which leads to the person becoming **overwhelmed**, resorting to **maladaptive behaviors** or remaining in a state of grief which **disallows progression** of the mourning process to completion.

Complicated grief may occur when any of the following are present:

___ Sudden or unanticipated death/loss

___ Death following a long illness

___ Loss of a child

___ A troubled pre-morbid relationship

___ Multiple losses

___ Violent death

___ Perceived issues of preventability or randomness

___ Mental illness prior to death/loss

___ Lack of social support

___ Feelings of guilt or resentment

___ No Closure

___ **YES TOTAL**

Even one of these factors is enough to say your grief is complicated. So, what does that mean for you and your grief experience? It may show why this experience carries so much emotion and may take years to feel a sense of acceptance and not feel overwhelmed. Clarifying this may help us feel more at peace. Specific options for healing can also become evident. Change and hope are on the horizon!

Chronic Grief

An on-going, prolonged experience with **no significant reduction in emotional distress**. Experienced **pain and sadness** that is **triggered by events**. Inability to move through the grief process due to on-going circumstances such as **chronic life issues or health conditions**.

____ Feeling stuck

____ Prolonged experience

____ Emotion triggered by events

____ Long term emotional distress

____ Chronic health problems

____ Long term life challenges

___**YES TOTAL**

After looking at this list, you may find your grief is chronic as well as complicated. The key word in this list is "on-going." If you continue to be triggered and feel overwhelmed, it's time to seek help. The 5WE's can be particularly helpful in creating movement through chronic grief.

Delayed Grief

Inability to experience loss *at this time.*

___ Timing

___ Family roles & responsibility

___ Age at Time of Loss

___ Substance Use

___ Emotional Instability

___ Previous Losses

___ Fear of loss of control

___ YES TOTAL

Is your grief delayed? Were you young and did not understand how to grieve? Were there complications in the timing of your loss? Did you delay due to taking charge or fear of being lost to your emotions? If yes, then grief is still waiting for you. The good news is that you know where you stand, are ready and can see clearly "what" you need to process!

Fully Alive

I will not die an unlived life.

I will not live in fear

of falling or catching fire.

I choose to inhabit my days,

to allow my living to open me,

to make me feel less afraid,

more accessible,

to loosen my heart

until it becomes a wing,

a torch, a promise.

I choose to risk my significance;

to live so that which came to me as seed,

goes to the next as blossom

and that which came to me a blossom,

goes on as fruit.

BY DAWNA MARKOVA
DawnaMarkova.com

CHAPTER 5

The Things You Can't Explain: Spiritual or Miraculous

Let's talk about what people don't talk about... what I call the "Unexplainable." Many of us have experiences after a loss that we cannot explain. It may be a sense of something/ someone, a dream, an event, or things we are quick to define as coincidences. You are not alone in this sometimes unexpected, surprising journey.

My personal story starts with my father...

> *To understand how my father left this world, you have to understand how his life began. He was number 10 of 11 children, and the youngest boy. Born at less than three pounds in the late 1930s, he was not supposed to live. But my Grandmother and the doctor who helped him into this world kept him alive and he grew from a fragile state to a wiry, mischievous little boy. He had a gift for music; before he hit his teens, he was playing with a jazz band that sneaked him into bars. He played trumpet, piano and sang.*

My Father had nine lives. He must have been part cat. He fell down a well. Later while trying to imitate his older brother smoking a cigarette, he used a firecracker and blew out all his teeth. He survived his childhood, went off to college, married my Mother, went off to war and made it back. Another life was scratched off when he contracted tuberculosis. I remember going to that scary hospital to visit him when he was skin and bones. He survived. I recall the front page of the local paper showing his car wrapped around a telephone pole after he was hit by a train. Yet he still clung to life and made it to the ripe old age of 80.

He liked living and having fun, he worked hard, studied hard and drank too much. He was prideful and could be self-absorbed. This self-focus showed in the way he left this world.

For me it started on an average day, nothing but blue sky and sunshine in Arizona while I drove off to work. My phone rang and the woman on the other end of the line from Adult Protective Services said "Your Father pulled a knife on a caregiver today. The agency will no longer be seeing him and he needs to move out of his Senior Living Apartment." That led to six weeks of calls and investigations, searching for benefits, and a new appropriate home for my Father whose dementia had increased along with his demanding attitude.

It was a whirlwind of effort. My Sister got him packed up, and moved him from Texas to Nevada. He went by car, followed by a U-Haul with the last of his belongings. He had his 80th birthday on the way and they stopped for an ice cream cone. He told me it tasted "pretty good," which in my Fathers language meant "excellent." While on the road I called my Father to say "Happy Birthday" and once again told him he was doing the right thing.

He arrived at what would be his new home on a Monday and that Friday my sister and I flew up to finish getting him settled in. All my work in this transition had been behind the scenes with doctors' calls, paperwork and admissions and when I saw him for the first time, he had deteriorated significantly. That stubborn prideful man told us on the way out the door that day that he was done. He meant it. One week later he was gone.

The day of my Father's funeral was a long one. It ended almost two months of struggle with making arrangements for care and moving him across the country so he could hopefully be happier with his environment and be closer to where my mother laid at rest. That evening I had the experience below and immediately reached for my laptop and began to write. I did not pause or stop to edit, it just poured from me. I wrote until I felt I was done. I have not changed one word of my original writing of "The Visit."

It was a fitful night of sleep, tossing and turning, my mind full of thoughts and memories. I couldn't seem to get comfortable and would doze off for short periods at a time only to find myself awakened by my heavy heart.

It was near dawn when I finally settled into a promising rest but a frightening dream appeared where I was being followed by lions and a panther. I tried to warn off the others around me but had difficulty finding my voice and at last got the words of danger from my throat as I turned to run.

I grew tired of the dream and wanted to wake and as I did, I felt a presence, one so familiar to me even with my eyes closed, sit on the bed beside me and put a gentle hand on my hip. As I became more aware, I knew it to be my Father.

Thinking that my mind was reaching for some comfort I almost dismissed it until I heard near my ear, a gentle kiss in the air. This sealed my knowing and left me with a wordless understanding that he was at peace, all was forgiven and that we would both be okay. I turned to look over my shoulder but no vision appeared as I began to cry. I cried for my Father, I cried for myself; for the relief of his struggle with his failing body and memory and for the gratitude of the visit and closure to the long month prior to chaos, frustration and exhaustion.

This is the ending of the story of my life with my Father...

I share this with you because so many people have experiences that they cannot put into a box of understanding. I share it because I know I am not alone. There are events that are not explainable. Spiritual experiences may be comforting or frightening and most of us do not talk about them. These experiences can shape our pain and our understanding, providing a sense of peace hard to find elsewhere and affecting our ability to move forward. My experience altered my course through grief in the most pleasant and helpful way. I had a true sense that my Father was at peace and that anything between us that caused strife was no longer significant.

Many others have had unexplainable or miraculous experiences yet feel uncomfortable sharing them with others. This is part of our spiritual experience with grief and loss. My experience helped soothe and validate my perspective. This topic and these experiences became, for me, a necessary part of this book. The more I share my experience, the more I hear that others have had similar experiences that were meaningful and prolific. This is as normal as breathing...

I continue to share to open the door for you to do the same. When I have shared my experience during workshops, others who want to share their story quite often approach me. I have had the privilege of hearing others' experiences and stories that come in all forms. You may hear or see something, have dreams, have a feeling or sense some kind of presence, or notice a symbol connecting you to a loved one. I don't believe in coincidences. You are not losing it! You are not alone.

Spirituality can be a sensitive topic for those in grief, although many of us have grown up with some sort of religious or spiritual foundation. These beliefs may not carry into your adulthood. As you grow, learn, and experience more of life, including the tragic events we have to bear, our spirituality may be challenged or shifted in a direction you might not have anticipated. It may be a new avenue to you. I believe it is BELIEF that is helpful and healing. It does not matter if your spiritual life revolves around going to church each Sunday, or if it is a Buddhist temple, synagogue, or a practice at home that you made your own. You may rely on the faith that the sun will rise each day and the Universe will smile down on you. You may believe that there is right and wrong that guides your life, or other principles giving you a spiritual foundation. No matter what this looks like in your life, belief seems to soothe us when our world is in crisis with grief and sorrow.

The Unexplainable is just another sign that there is more out there than we can understand. There is no need to force logic upon your experiences. It does not create any additional peace. Go with it, notice what is happening around you. The signs presented can enable you to move forward with your grieving and healing. At times, our heads can get in the way. We may try to rationalize and make sense of the unexplainable, attempting to force the experience into place, only further complicating our grief.

Clients often tell me they had a dream, or heard a song on the radio with a message that "I am okay." I have heard of butterflies following someone around or people seeing a saying on a sign that was something a loved one was constantly preaching. When these spiritual experiences are discussed, clients may smile, seem peaceful, or have goosebumps. Trusting your gut, and staying out of your head can allow sharing and belief that you have been touched by something you cannot measure. Again, what you believe in or do not believe in does not matter; it is most important that you believe in something, anything.

Sometimes it is small things. One young woman had three significant losses and did not know whom to focus on in her grief work. My name, Gigi, made the decision for her. Her Grandmother was one of the three influential figures in her life and her nickname was Gigi.

During a workshop, I recall a young man who lost his best friend. He had a raven tattoo on his arm because his friend had always been fascinated by these birds. There were big trees outside the windows of the meeting room and ravens, or crows, that had taken over these trees. They were noisy and each morning we would speak up to be heard over them. He would say, "That is my friend Devon." On the final day of the workshop, he read his final writing, providing a peaceful vibe over the whole room. Then he said "Listen!" All the birds were gone. He took it as a sign he no longer had to hold onto the heaviness of his grief. Once he shared his story, several other people were excited about sharing too. This normalized the experience and led to a workshop group that was more open, trusting and supportive.

Rex, lost his best friend Phil, his "Buddy." They had spent hours working on cars in his garage and had many deep conversations. Phil loved the rain and would just stop to be silent and listen to it. Rex told me on the last morning of the workshop, that he had had difficulty doing his homework for that day. He had stopped and started writing several times, but then it started to rain. Rex said "I have been here for 45 days now, this is the first time it has rained, I took it as a sign that my writing was complete."

In the same group was a young woman who lost her Auntie. Her Auntie Denise loved the band "Toto" and particularly the song "Africa." After the workshop, I was making the hour and a half drive home, listening to music. It wasn't the first or second song, but "Africa" was the third song and it was followed by a beautiful song by Bruce Hornsby called "Mandolin Rain." There is a lovely line in this song: "Listen to the tears roll, down my face as she turns to go⊠" A warm smile came over me as I sang along and I said hello to Phil and Auntie Denise:)

During one workshop Kara told the story of her Father. They had been very close. He had lost his battle with cancer two years before. Their relationship had been strained during a period when she lost herself to opiate use and depression. Her Father had given her a ring which she always wore on her hand or on a chain around her neck. During the course of her addiction, she had moved around a lot and realized at some point that she had lost her ring. Kara searched everywhere she could think of, but did not find it. Then she returned home to live for a while and tried to pull her life back together, but after a painful day had decided to use again. She took some pills, then decided that she was tired and done with this struggle. She took the pill bottle to her bedside and lay down, planning on taking the whole bottle, but the pills spilled onto the floor. As she began to scoop up those pills, she found the ring from her father under the bed. Instead of swallowing pills, Kara called for help and was in treatment the same week. Her Father had come through for her even after he was gone.

Not everyone will have an "unexplainable" moment. Others may look on with envy, wishing they could find this kind of reassurance or release. We don't always have these types of experiences, and this is not the only road to peace. The examples above show these experiences come in many forms. Like little reminders of a loved one's favorite songs, shows, or activities, look for the small things as well as profound moments. Some of my clients have created an experience by seeing a psychic. This is another option. You may have had unexplainable moments with a past loss, but not with every loss. Overall, what is within your power is to remain open to the possibility. If you do not have an encounter, that is okay. It is not the only way to find reassurance and healing. Reassurance may come from your spiritual base, your emotional tie, or deep knowing of your loved one. Whatever your spiritual belief is, embrace it, use it to create comfort. The "Unexplainable" is another experience that some feel when suffering with loss.

CHAPTER 6

The Roles
We Take & Why

Grief slips into more life circumstances than we can count. You might be enjoying a typical day, full of challenges at work, managing your family and trying to balance everything else in life that requires attention. Tragedy seems to strike on the most ordinary days, when we least expect it, as was the case with the loss of my Father. It was an ordinary work day, my schedule full of clients to be seen, mail to sort and a list of things to follow up on that just kept coming. I did not expect that on this sun-shiny day, while singing and driving to the office, the phone would ring and my world would shift and lead to the beginning of the end for my Father.

The circumstances can be a set-up for how we feel, function and react to our grief as well as the roles we assume. Our roles may be clarified by questions such as these: Where are you in the birth order of your family? Who carries the responsibility for power of attorney? Are you the oldest child or the most available person, because you are retired? Are you between jobs or living a more flexible lifestyle? Do you live in proximity to your loved one? Answers to these questions affect the role you may take when there is tragedy within your support system. When I use the word "family" I speak in the broad sense. Some of us have friends, neighbors, mentors, and bosses who are our most treasured family/support system.

The strength of these relationships plays into our roles. Are you best friends, or has your relationship been strained for years? Have you been the designated caregiver or are you the one with less time and more ability to help with care financially? Have you been caring for your loved one for a long time with resentment growing as you became exhausted? Maybe you had a recent loss and are in the midst of healing. There are many scenarios that shape our roles. There are as many grieving styles as there are individuals. Each of us has walked a different path leading us to today; our relationships and roles with each loss may be very different. We may think we know how we will react. However, it can be unpredictable. From one loss to another, your role can change. With what we know about complicated, chronic and delayed grief, this makes sense.

Our reaction to loss can be shaped by our roles in the family/support system. There may be expectations for you to act in a certain way, take the lead, or be a silent participant. We hold expectations for ourselves, but other family members may see us in a different light. I watched and worked with patients and families for over 20 years in a hospital setting. I had the gift of being present and supporting patients and family members as they embarked on this journey of grieving. There were similarities, roles that would show up again and again, and there were also uniqueness. Here are several primary roles I saw repeatedly.

The Responsible Person

You know who you are! You're the one! The one who everyone always turns to, the one who pulls it all together, organizes everything. Perhaps this is a natural position, or even a comfortable position for you. It could be just the opposite. You have these skills and abilities, but don't enjoy being put in such a position. This may lead to resentment as you put off what you need in order to take care of the bigger picture. You may also be the perfectionist or the pressure-driven person in your family.

My client Faye is an example. She is the oldest of five children. When her Mother was diagnosed with cancer with six months to live, Faye's reaction was to put on her "take charge" hat, fire up her perfectionism, begin researching the diagnosis, options for treatment, and finding the best physicians in the area to treat her Mother.

Being the responsible family member may seem like the perfect (pun intended) role to scratch that itch in circumstances that can otherwise feel out of control or helpless. Some of us are just built to "Do." Some of us need something to do. Direction can elude us when we are anticipating or in the throes of loss. The responsible person tries to make things manageable for everyone else. The disadvantage of this role is that the responsible person often puts their needs on the back burner. There is the thought that after I take care of the accounts, the service arrangements, etc., I will get back to thinking about and caring for myself and my own grief needs. This may lead to chronic or delayed grief. Grief may show up later from these stuffed feelings that have gone unexpressed, or distance us from other relationships due to underlying fear of losing again. Faye told me these derailed her from her grief and led her to seek help.

Taking on this responsible role may not be a conscious decision. You may be on automatic pilot in this role as you consult with medical professionals, coordinate family arrivals and accommodations, and find all the necessary insurance information, and legal documents. This puts your other life responsibilities on hold. The children may be cared for by others, bills may stack up, and your personal health may suffer while eating and sleeping becomes a suggestion, not a necessity. I have heard family members say that they "do what has to be done," or often that there is no one else to do it. Sometimes there is no choice, or at least you may feel there is none.

Unfortunately, the responsible person may not get back to their own self-care. They may minimize their needs for time to grieve, leading to the complication of delayed grief. I have heard the cries of delayed grief, the agony of what has been waiting for months or years to be expressed in a genuine way.

When my Mother died, I stepped into this role. She had struggled with colon cancer and had a clean bill of health until three years later when there was a recurrence with metastasis. After years of working in a hospital ICU setting, it was a natural position for me to fill. I understood the medical terminology and could ask key questions that made it clear that her prognosis was grave. I was able to turn to my family with compassion and explain that we needed to take her off the ventilator, all of us knowing this is what she would want. I have always looked back on this time, feeling grateful that I could step in and do this last important thing for her.

The Clown

Best thought of as the Entertainer, the Clown is the person who wants to keep things light. Although they may be in the reality of what is happening, they would prefer to focus on positive and happier times and memories. This person may enjoy telling stories of their loved ones' escapades that bring about warm feelings and even laughter. This take on loss may be healthy, yet sometimes uncomfortable for others.

The person in this role can provide much needed relief from the intensity in the room with their light hearted attitude and stories. Of all the roles, this one tends to go untaken, maybe due to expectations or a sense of external or internal pressures to behave in a certain way. Tolerance for this style can be questionable.

When my best friend Kristoff's Mother was put on Hospice and sent home to live her last days, we, as a family, had the most wonderful experience. I would come by after work to check on her at home. She was often sleeping as she became weaker. One day I arrived to find Wilma wide awake, talking and alert. I have seen this rallying before, near the end of life. I called Kristoff and said "Call everyone, get them all here as soon as possible." As we all gathered around Wilma's bed, she talked about how she used to dance, being young and carefree.

We shared funny stories and good memories. There was laughter and we celebrated her life in those moments. I feel so blessed that we all had that time. I don't think she would have wanted it any other way.

The Clowns are at risk of having delayed grief if they use this light hearted stance as a shield to avoid heavier or painful feelings. Such behavior can be a way of avoiding the pain, or even magical thinking that the loss is not permanent. If this is you, identifying this role and reflecting on delayed grief information in Chapter 4 may be helpful.

The Emotionally Overwhelmed

If you are an emotional person with intense expressions of feelings and moods, either happy or sad, you may fall into the emotionally overwhelmed category when it comes to a loss. As with all grieving styles, the circumstances of the loss will influence your emotional stance. Others may also identify the emotionally overwhelmed person in the support system as "the sensitive one." This person may become so distraught it may be unbearable for them to remain present and stay in the fold. They may require medical assistance or medications to calm them. There may be outpourings of emotion from anger to sobbing as they embrace the heartbreak of the loss.

When we are experiencing intense emotion, especially over a prolonged period of time, we may need to leave this role and move to being Numbed Out. Being numbed out is the most frequent choice and gives us a chance to recharge, a much-needed break to feel more in control, clear-headed, and functional. The emotionally overwhelmed grieving style has the smallest chance of delayed grief as people with this style are full-on present with what they are feeling. However, their grief may become chronic if they are unable to move toward healing. They may experience some of the effects we discussed in Chapter 2 such as career or personal relationship struggles. They may seek counseling without identifying that the problem was grief. This leads back to why I ask the Magic Question. The Emotionally Overwhelmed may also trigger the next role, the Caretaker into action.

For Claire, the pain was immeasurable. To lose her twin Sister Caren struck her in the heart harder than anything had so far in her lifetime and she crumbled. As her sister slipped away, she began to cry with a deep wounding sound permeating the room. Once it started, she could not stop and had to be consoled and escorted out of the room. The intensity of her emotion lasted for weeks. Just when she felt she was feeling a moment of control, the realization would hit her again and the tears would flow. Claire had only fitful bouts of sleep and would only eat when someone put food in front of her. This went on for weeks before her feelings eased and became more manageable.

The Caretaker

The Caretaker is the person in the support system who cares for everyone else. Their attention and concern focus on the needs for support and soothing of those around them. Caretakers may become overwhelmed with the needs of others. They may have a natural tendency toward codependent behavior as they are singularly focused on other's needs. Codependency, as it relates to this situation, is putting everyone else's physical and emotional needs before your own and even sacrificing your own needs to make sure others are cared for. If you are the caregiver in your support system, a significant amount of time and emotional energy may be directed outside yourself to help others manage their grief. This puts your feelings on the back burner, with the promise of "I will take care of myself later." Unfortunately, sometimes that "later" does not come, or comes years down the road. The Caretaker, like the Responsible Person, may have delayed grief because of the focus outside of self.

These grieving roles are not exclusive. The Responsible person and the Caretaker may be one and the same. If you are doubling up on roles, you might be straddling the line between taking care of the business of loss while keeping an eye out for who may need your attention. Caretakers are not usually the best at delegating or asking for help. Those in this role often have delayed grief because their focus is outside of themselves and the last person the caretaker takes care of is themselves. These roles can harbor the other underlying issues discussed in Chapter 2, like codependency, anxieties, traumatic history, that may lead to seeking counsel.

Patricia was the one everyone turned to with a question, whether for a recipe, the latest health tip, or response to crisis. Pat was "the person." She had a long history of worrying about how everyone was managing. She would fret about even small things, not wanting to offend anyone and strived for every gathering to be perfect. She would call people afterwards to make sure they got home safely and had a good time. Therefore, it was no surprise that, when her closest cousin Sydney was in a terrible car accident, she took the lead to make sure everyone was okay. Pat sat at his bedside endless hours and would encourage others to go home and get some rest. "No" was not in her vocabulary. Since she was the "go to" person, she was on the run taking care of whatever needs people had. By the end of this journey, Patricia was completely exhausted and had not spent any time considering her own feelings of grief. Her journey toward healing from this loss was just to begin.

The Numbed Out

Being numbed out may be a sign of shock or denial. But it can be a primary coping skill for some. This person may seem detached, even lost, at the time of a crisis. They may have to be told what to do or may remove themselves from the event because they are unable to participate or tolerate participation. It's self-preservation in action. Our bodies often need time to catch up with what we are experiencing to avoid being overwhelmed. Numbing out is one way of accomplishing this. Others may numb out intentionally with, alcohol, medication or other substances to reduce the emotional intensity they are feeling. It is also common for those who tend to be emotionally overwhelmed to move to a numbed-out phase for self-preservation from too much emotion.

Underlying dysfunction may surface after a loss that makes it impossible for the griever to maintain their outward facade that all is okay. Their anxieties or depression may flare, leading them to seek support. Addictions or past mental health struggles previously processed and stabilized in recovery may be activated, causing a relapse.

Raylene shared in a workshop that she lost both parents over a short period of time. She had been struggling with alcohol abuse for years and had finally hit her stride in her recovery when she lost her father, Frank, suddenly. He was diagnosed with cancer and three months later he was gone. This sent Raylene over the emotional edge and she once again turned to alcohol to avoid the feelings bubbling to the surface. Being numb was the logical solution as this is how she had handled tragedy in the past. With alcohol on board, she did not have to think or feel about the loss of her father and the loss of her mother, Estell, that closely followed. Raylene spent months feeling numb and avoiding her pain until she reached for help and entered a treatment facility.

These grieving styles and roles are not exclusive and several people may share the same role at the same time. You may move from one role to another during the course of a grief experience. When looking at a variety of losses in life, you may react completely differently to each one.

Understanding how you react to grief, based on the roles you gravitate toward, may help you identify what support you need based on your history, personality and experience with loss. Some roles can cause you to delay your grief, struggle with chronic grief, or have other complications discussed in Chapters 2-4. All this information is building a framework to you understanding you, and preparing you for the work ahead in Section 2.

Another complication with these roles is our lack of tolerance for how others experience and react to grief. We also judge ourselves. We seem to have a place in the back of our minds that says, "This is how you do it!" If others don't fall in line with those expectations another message pops up saying, "You are doing it wrong!" I remember this sweet older couple when I was working in the Neuro ICU. Betty was 92 years old as was her husband, Stan. Betty had a severe bleed in her brain. As soon as visiting hours started, Stan would come and sit by her bedside, holding her hand and talking to her. Each evening the staff would shoo him out, telling him to go home and get some rest.

One day the doctor and I had to tell him that Betty would not survive, it was a matter of days. Stan and Betty had been married for over 60 years. They spent one night apart in all that time, on the night she gave birth to their daughter Carla, who passed away several years earlier. One day as Stan was sitting by the bedside, he suddenly stood up, held Betty's hand and said "Bye, bye Betty." Stan walked out of the ICU, then out of the hospital, and he never came back. A couple days later I overheard a conversation at the Nurses Station. They were talking about Stan. "It is so horrible that he has left her here all alone." I butted in, saying, "Please stop! You don't understand; this is probably the hardest thing he has ever had to do in his life. He could not bear to sit by and watch his love of 60 years slip away. He is doing the best he can. Please don't judge."

It is so easy for us to fall into the trap of judgement. It may take a conscious effort to respect other people's grieving styles and roles. Staying out of your head will help to squash thoughts like, "She's not sad enough, " "They are over the top emotionally," or "He is not present with his feelings." Beware: while you judge others, they may judge you as well. Remember, as in the story of Betty and Stan, we do not know all the life experiences making each griever who they are and why they react to a death the way they do. For all we know, they may have discussed this kind of ending scenario in detail.

The judgement in the story above is one of the things you don't expect when grieving. Chapter 3 discusses the pain, overwhelming feelings and expression of emotions in this journey to healing, the limbo we feel as we sit between the heaviness and the hope that recovery to some normality is coming. Be kind and show compassion to yourself and others around you. Thoughtful awareness is key in preventing this kind of stumbling block to family and support systems as they come together and work toward healing.

CHAPTER 7

The Gifts You Don't Expect

You may be thinking, "Okay, I was following her up until this point, but what could possibly be good about, or a gift in this painful experience I am going through?" Hang in there with me just a bit longer and I'll lay it out for you. You have to look and search, but gifts are there, although they may not be obvious, as we struggle through the turmoil. Seeking these gifts is important. They can accelerate healing and help ease the pain of loss. Some gifts overlap. One pearl of wisdom can create a string of insights and gifts. Gifts keep giving and can bless your life and those around you.

This is another side to moving through a loss. Questions and feelings may lead to decisions and actions you have been stalling on for months or years. Loss may also create some positive energy to "Do." You will notice the overlap as you read through these gift categories. You have likely heard many times that all our experiences have value. Grief is no exception. Sometimes it is in the pain and challenges of our lives that create the most movement and clarity.

A poem that I am fond of speaks to this idea:

Sorrow

Our sorrow is the other face of love,

for we only mourn what we deeply care for....
The sorrow, grief and rage you feel

is the measure of your humanity and your

evolutionary maturity.

As your heart breaks open

there will be room for the world

to heal.

BY JOANNA MACY

The concept of gifts in grief first became evident to me when I was working in the hospital. There were periods of time when I was present for multiple patient deaths in a very short period of time. It was overwhelming for me. After I focused my compassion and attention on the patient and family, I paused to reflect on the experience, the patient, and what I knew of them and their life. Then I would reflect on my own life, and my purpose.

A strong overarching message became clear to me, "Life is precious," almost immediately followed by "Live fully and live now!" This changed the way I viewed all aspects of my life. It has been years since I experienced these influences, so it's hard to explain the intensity of their impact on me. Values, priorities, and relationships were shaped based on the precious moments I spent with patients and their families. They influence me today. Hidden gems may be left in each of the areas below.

Self-Examination

A rock from the ground looks nothing like a diamond until an amazing amount of force is placed upon it. The intense pressure transforms it into that brilliant stone. Such is the way of our lives. The pain and sadness of grief can make it difficult to see anything hopeful or positive. This is a common occurrence. Several key encouraging things can happen when we move through grief. First, we become more present in our lives, to what is around us and people important to us. It may feel like an awakening. This may lead to questions and feelings carrying you toward decisions and actions you may have been avoiding for months or years. It may create some positive energy to "do."

We may ask, "Who am I now without this person in my life?" This may be the first time in years you have had this kind of deep reflection. When grieving, life may seem to pause and you notice thoughts and feelings you have not made the time for, or paid close attention to, in the recent past. Questions can arise like: "Who am I becoming because of this grief experience?" "What is really important?" How am I living or am I just getting by?" "Is this all there is?" Positive energy related to loss could inspire this time of reflection. The need to define or redefine yourself, the questions "Who am I and where am I going?" leads to a desire to explore.

Analyzing our health and a hypersensitivity to aging can be another part of this self-examination. Some of us rush to the doctor to check that A1C level we have been avoiding for the last year, not knowing that our loss has ignited this visit. We may start the nutrition and exercise plan we have been "trying" to do for the last few months. After a loss, the realization that life is short and needs to be lived takes center stage. We are left behind, but often with the gifts of a renewed sense of purpose, determination, and presence. We may have been bestowed the gifts of awareness and connection. Grab hold and allow these gifts to direct you and sprout hope and determination.

Something about loss forces self-examination and gives us the opportunity to pause and dig deep. I have made big life decisions based on my shift in perspective after losing a loved one. I have no regrets, that I can remember.

The Shift

There is a shift caused by the pain of loss that may lead to awareness that what was once important and the focus of life, may now feel empty and meaningless. Or, it may open avenues for more passion and direction. This change may offer a wider view of life. This new perspective can be temporary, lasting weeks or months, and come on with a fierce attitude. Or, it may gain power as time goes by. The shift may build on itself as you understand and recalculate how you feel about various aspects of life.

Career paths, how we spend our leisure time, our relationships, and how we manage self-care, can all shift. Our work lives may have seemed satisfactory or just necessary before a loss. But as we grieve, we may find that "good enough" is no longer acceptable. This is a time to reflect on where you envisioned your career path would lead. Old hopes and the fire that accompanies them may re-ignite. You may feel emboldened to speak out and stand up for things important to you and refresh your original passion around your field of work. You may decide to do something new, take a surprising leap of faith, and feel anything is possible.

You may have spent hours on an interest or hobby that seemed fulfilling, with a garage or closet full of the supplies and equipment needed to feed the fun and fuel the interest. This shift may rekindle an interest or you may find it does not have that same pull. Feeling uninspired to make time to indulge in activities that have been set aside can be a product of our grief experience. Grief brings rethinking and reinventing priorities and interests.

Prior to loss, your time off may have seemed to float by while just trying to catch your breath from a long week of work and responsibilities. The shift's positive force may bring more value and presence to the time you have for self-care, friends and family. Connecting with others, hobbies and interests can lose their pull or draw us in like a yoyo. We may not even notice the shift, like a silent message guiding you to think or do things differently.

At times you may find yourself literally or figuratively, dreaming of things you would like to do, following an old passion or feeling the need to do something with more purpose or more in line with making life better for yourself and those you care about. This redefining and rediscovering who you are after a loss is truly a gift.

> *"Living vs. Surviving:*
> *we are not here*
> *to just 'get by.'"*
>
> ~ GV

Connection & Relationships

The gift of connection is a prominent gift from loss. Who is important becomes clear. It can be a natural sorting of priorities on an unconscious level. Maybe the realization that there is no time to waste which prompts us to redefine the bonds with people and let go of old grudges. We no longer want to spend time with people who don't serve our well-being and we embrace even tighter those who do. Maybe time is the key message. As we grieve, we know and see its limits and value.

There may be a need for contact and heightened connection to those we love, and a need to say "I love you" or "You are important to me." We stop taking our relationships and our opportunities for granted. Relationships that faded may be re-evaluated with questions, "Did I let this go for some petty reason?" or "Does what happened in the past matter to me anymore?" We contemplate if there is ample value to rekindle the bond: "Am I missing out on a relationship that provides joy, peace or connection in life?"

Improving an impaired connection may come from your heart's encouragement. Some people in our support systems who are important to us may have fallen off our radar and we haven't made the time to maintain contact. These neglected friends or family members may find their way into your schedule with renewed interest in the happenings of their lives.

Many of us have friends, associates, and even that second cousin that we keep in the loop of our lives... just because. It may seem like the right thing to do as there are unwritten rules within the family or group expecting us to do so. We may have "made up" the necessity to keep in touch because we always included Aunt Joan, or we can't not invite Tim from accounting to the gathering. We may re-evaluate with a new sense of what do "I" need and want in this life, more than what others expect or find acceptable.

We only have so much time to give and we want it to be high quality. We want to be present and involved in what we "choose." In the end, we pick and choose where our attention and energy should go. We are bolder. We look out for ourselves and those we love with a clearer intent and a sense of protection. We come back to the message of "I don't want to waste time and energy." This can be an uncomfortable realization, or we may feel brazen in this philosophy and new way of viewing life.

After Monica died, I had an intense desire to contact all my loved ones to say, "Our friendship and this loving relationship is very important to me." I think it was a desire not to have any regrets. I followed through. I called all of my "peeps" to have this conversation. I also asked if we could get together soon and scheduled time for lunch, a walk, or a relaxed afternoon at home. As I met with each loved one, I made sure to say the words and mean this message with all the depth I could show. Then I took a picture of us together so I could hold that memory. I was very busy with social plans for about three months! I thank Monica for shining a light on the gifts of love I have in my life.

Cherished Memories

Another direction our thoughts may go is to look back and examine our life journey with our loved ones. We reflect on the life and experiences we had with our loved ones, the time spent together, the adventures and the challenges. There is a new level of cherishing when we explore these memories. One of the most comforting things someone can do for me when I am grieving is to share with me their favorite memories of my loved one.

It can be bolstering and our warm and happy feelings travel to the surface. It helps us move through grief. Working as a team may have been an important part of your life with your loved one in a professional capacity, or the joy of having a like-minded explorer to travel with to isolated places around the world. Time away from routine life, exploring and having adventures, can develop special memories.

Memories of scary times when you needed your loved one's support or they needed your reassurance as you traversed life's twists, turns, speed bumps and momentous happenings, all influence how you will feel after a loss. There are happy joyful times, recalling laughter until you felt you would both fall over, the joys of celebration, and the unity of sharing ,special occasions with someone who really knows your journey, or simply gets who you are and who you are becoming.

Memories of panicky situations where you needed someone solid, stable and rooted by your side to reassure you or to make you feel safe as you worked through a challenge can lead to feeling alone without that person's anchoring. The accomplishments you tackled together or felt you could not have reached without the other remind you of the richness of the bond you had.

Whatever the circumstances, you made it through together and you made it through as a team, with a focused effort with an open heart and mind. Even as you battled to get your point across and stood your ground to be understood and influence decisions, you were connecting. This is what we call "relationships." Misunderstandings, laughing so hard you cry, sharing joys, regrets, sorrows and embarrassments are all part of the connection. These memories create a special, unique and irreplaceable history. No one else can step into that role or be that person.

We may remember some challenging memories differently, while stories that irritated us in the past no longer seem irritating or significant. They may now seem charming and a fond reminder of the quirkiness of our loved one. The stubbornness may now be remembered as determination or passion and doting may seem like warmth and caring. Our tendency is to see the best in others and the best in our interactions with loved ones so that circumstances that once challenged us may be rearranged in our memories.

Others may even say how mad or how hurt you were when that happened, but now the story has been re-written in your mind. We choose to remember in a way that is more pleasant, acceptable, or respectful of those that are gone.

Anger to Action

Most of us tap into anger as we grieve, especially with tragic losses leaving us to feel the world has been unfair. We can use angry energy to help create amazing impacts in the lives of those we love, our community, or society. Some shy from anger like it's an ugly emotion, but anger directed, can create purpose and drive to change laws, rules of the road, medical practice, increase awareness of social issues, or inspire programs affecting many families and communities. So, this gift born of tragedy can become hope.

Think about it, the last time you were highly motivated to do something, experience something, or take a leap of faith, did it come from slow calculated thought or did you just get fired up, irritated or intolerant of some injustice or circumstance? Did frustration or angry energy make the difference? I have watched parents, friends, and co-workers take action following a tragic loss of a loved one, when they felt changes could prevent this from happening to someone else. Their actions might include bringing more awareness to mental health, bullying, advocacy programs, and all kinds of support services. This directed energy can create changes in awareness, policy and availability of support services becoming a gift for another person's loved one.

The world should make way and watch out as those of us who are left behind put energy into making the world a better place for the rest of us. I thank them.

Recognition of Mortality

When I met with my client Liz who lost her Brother Theo two months prior, she said she had been having "uncomfortable thoughts." I coaxed more detail from her. She had been thinking about her life and wondering how long she had to live it. It can be scary. You might have more than uncomfortable thoughts--you might experience nightmares. I told her this was a normal reaction to grief and we had a healthy discussion about how she wanted to spend the years of life ahead of her. Liz said she felt selfish thinking of herself at a "time like this," and I reiterated that it is natural to turn our thoughts and focus inward after a loss.

When our world changes in such a powerful way, we may recognize our fragility and how quickly things can change. I don't believe this is selfish, I call it being "self-full," a healthy expression of self-focus. When we start with ourselves, we have a strong influence on healing while grieving, and later meeting other challenges in life.

Liz embraced this philosophy, and after normalizing and understanding these thoughts, troublesome thoughts and dreams began to diminish from being scary and began taking shape as more future-directed actions. Liz was able to use this "reframe" to be more present in life and sought increased fulfillment and joy by living in the present.

Grief can lead us to the most amazing opportunity any of us can have—to live, not just survive. Loss can make these distinctions clearer. This kind of reflection and presence is a gift.

Charitable Works

Giving can be a path to healing. If you can make some of your loved one's dreams and passions come alive, it feels purposeful. My client Sergio was a young, wiry, and antsy guy. He had difficulty sitting for a 50-minute session. He was all about "doing." So, we spent a session just talking about some things he could do that would make the memory of his best friend Jack, who was like a brother to him, stay alive. Sergio really lit up; his already intense energy hyper-focused on creative ideas. Jack was into books and didn't mind the title of nerd. He preferred reading over most other activities, and would keep Sergio on the phone explaining the plot of the latest book or some interesting fact he learned about history.

So, Sergio decided to start volunteering to read to young kids at the local library, one of Jack's favorite hangouts. When I saw Sergio after his first time at the library, he talked endlessly about the kids and how he enjoyed it, all the time feeling that Jack was right there, reading over his shoulder. I think this gift was as much for Sergio as Jack.

Something about giving in the face of loss brings about healing. Think of your loved one's interests, pet causes and what they would stand up for due to their inability to remain silent: ideas of charitable works will come to your mind. This is a healthy place to express some of your grieving energy. As I continue to write, I can almost hear Monica's voice saying, "You are doing great, keep going!" This is my charitable work as well as my passion. Her voice sparks the energy I have about writing, and sharing experiences that may touch others in healing ways.

Pack Only What You Need

When William came in for his fourth session, he came with an agenda. He said, "I want to know why things that have bothered me so much in the past now seem to be no big deal." He had been experiencing relaxation and calm around topics that used to stir either his passion, opinions or indignation. Lately, he noticed he would let things go, not getting overly involved or overwhelmed emotionally. When asked, he agreed this shift occurred a few weeks after his roommate and best friend Dale drowned. I said this was something observed in many clients during the initial phases of grieving.

There seems to be an adjustment in priorities, and decision making. Some decisions now seem so clear and easy. You might have been vacillating over them for months, feeling lost in what you REALLY want to do or how you TRULY feel about a relationship, topic, or life direction.

It reminds me of packing for a trip. Before the shift in priorities, you may have ruminated over what you should bring for every possible, and even unlikely, scenario. But now you pack only what you need. This approach minimizes additional stress or regrets. If you forgot something, you'll simply pick it up when you get there.

This clarity of sight seems to be reflected in several of the other gifts. There may be a continual evaluation of not wasting time or energy with little things, or details that we are not invested in. We do not want to be bothered as we see the big picture. Life and time are precious. So, we pack only what we need, taking a pass on the fretting, over analyzing and preparing for the outside chance of snow in Hawaii. Loss of a loved one leave us with sharp sight and obvious conclusions. I believe it is the gift of deep reflection and clarity.

Here Comes the Light

We are coming to the end of the first part of our journey together. You have done the deep work of reflecting and gathering insights as we have walked through the knowledge and built a foundation of understanding for yourself and your thoughts, feelings and even wrong steps taken on this journey through grief.

We have looked at the "why?" and the depth of your sorrow, plus your challenges or "uphill battles" as you reach for healing. You have felt the waves of grief as they wash over you, as the Old Guy says. We considered the unexplainable and the grief we may not yet have seen or identified as the basis of our pain. "Gifts from grief" sounds paradoxical, and perhaps unbelievable, but there are ways to experience them. But doing so requires engaging in another paradox, and diving in deeper to the pain and grief to get the most healing out of it. This is the work of *The Five Written Expressions of Grief*™. As David said in the Foreword, it will take you from the depths to the heights. It is time to take this next step built on the strength of your knowing, the connection to your feelings, and the desire for healing. I think you are ready! Let's get started in Section Two.

You are left behind, but often with the gifts of a renewed sense of purpose, determination, and connection. Be present to notice the gifts bestowed. Awareness is key.

"The best revenge is living fully"

~ GV

The Five
Written
Expressions
of Grief

Introduction to The Five Written Expressions

The Power of the Pen: Journaling as a Tool

I have been journaling off and on for years. It started with a teenage diary, recounting the details of my day, the frustration with math, ugh or my crush on the boy down the street. It helped me sort things out, make sense of my feelings and sometimes even solve a problem or explore a bright idea. As I grew older, journaling has allowed me to unearth everything from my fears to secret desires. It was good for me and provided release and/or relief. So, I felt it would be good for others and I have made it a point to include journaling as homework for my clients. One base principle in my practice is that homework is beneficial and moves clients more quickly through whatever strife they have come to divulge. Everyone seems in a hurry for healing these days and I am often asked the question "How many sessions do you think this will take?" The first homework after that question usually relates to patience.

As I have worked with clients and patients over the years, I had a growing desire to find a way to help them move along and toward self-discovery. I came up with things for them to do, think about, say or take care of old business or burdensome "to-do's" that would lead to some relief of grief and movement toward healing and peace. So, I formulated a plan. Why not write your way through the feelings that help you to remember and cherish the relationship of your loved one while relinquishing feelings of guilt, responsibility and regrets. *The Five Written Expressions of Grief*™ was born of these thoughts.

Works previously done by Elizabeth Kubler-Ross with her Five Stages of Grief gave us a foundation for understanding grief and loss. I wrote earlier about Elizabeth Kubler-Ross and her substantial contributions to our understanding of grief/loss and death/dying. I stood on the foundation she left and this helped me understand and interpret the experiences of grief/loss I see in my clients and patients. Another contributor to development of the 5WE's is Beverly Ryan, who worked with Hospice patients and their families, looking for ways to communicate toward the end of life. She encouraged discussion of things unsaid as well as sharing love and gratitude for the person's effect on their life. Beverly developed "The Four Gifts" families have used to discuss anticipated losses.

I was inspired by these amazing women and related their work to my work in the hospitals and later on in my office with clients struggling with complicated grief. My voice will now be added to those you have just read about. My perspective is based on years working with patients and families. These observations widened and shaped my perspective on death, dying, grief and loss. This has left me with a certain comfort with the subject and led to a calling to create this therapeutic process.

I found those seeking help had usually been wrestling with their loss for a long period of time or they felt stuck in certain feelings and the intensity of those feelings were not lessening over time. Some clients didn't know what to expect from grief and put undue pressure on themselves to move through at a pace only seen in films. I wanted to find a way to answer the unanswered questions, help clients feel and move through difficult feelings, and embrace memories of their loved one. *The Five Written Expressions of Grief*™ were born from this desire.

The Five Written Expressions or as I call them, the 5WE's, are a writing/journaling process to help identify where you are in the healing process and assist in expressing feelings. It will help you embrace the fond memories along with the challenges of your relationship. Memories of events and stories you have not thought about in years may spring to mind to be captured in your journal. You are building a keepsake.

The Five Written Expressions has been fine-tuned over the years as I watched clients work through it, and saw what seems to ease the pain and promote healing. It has been like a painting where I continually add layers of color and texture, to bring it further to life. I have learned from those who have used the process and provided feedback on what they related to most, of what brought about that ah-ha moment or a sense of resolve. I used the process myself when I lost my dear friend Monica and again after my Father died.

The key is not simply in the writing but in the sharing. The sharing can be done in a therapeutic setting, with another loved one or in a workshop group. Being able to share the experience of love and pain, fears and sorrows with others who have been in that space is powerful. There is power in the voicing of your writing. Hearing yourself read those words may bring up more emotion than you might anticipate as you breathe life into the words. After reading out-loud a client may say, "I didn't cry when I wrote this..." or "I was not expecting to be so emotional..." What I notice as an observer is the attachment to the experience, ownership that this is MY story.

When we no longer distance ourselves from grief and pain we begin to heal. My motto is "The healing is through the feelings." Awareness and being present in this way are key. It might seem easier to avoid the reality of loss or minimize it and hope that it will go away naturally. Those who do not like to write will need to get over that in order to find the jewel that is waiting for you! Writing by hand is key, it creates connection to your thoughts and words.

One of the most amazing experiences in my work is when I do a workshop on grief and loss. I am in a room with four to twelve people there to learn, share their stories and shed their burdens. To hear the amount of loss just one of these people has had can be heartbreaking. That message echoed over and over as each participant talked about their losses, the things they witnessed and the pain that does not seem to pass. Here is the good part; I get to be part of their healing as they comfort each other, receive validation of their feelings and start to let go of the heaviness as I guide the group through the process. It leaves me with a sense of awe at their openness, vulnerability and courage, and we leave the room together as a group who have gone through something very personal and special.

When it is done, I am spent. I sit in the gift that I have been given to be part of their journeys and it takes me a day or more to be able to refuel and rejuvenate. It takes an incredible amount of energy to hold that sacred place for the group, but I absolutely love it, I am in my element. Then I do it all over again.

I don't sweat, okay so I seldom sweat. I can do a good hour of cardio and only politely glisten. :) I remember conducting my first workshop at a treatment facility in the San Francisco Bay area. I previously came to the facility for a referent visit and met this incredible team of professionals doing great work with those struggling with trauma and addiction. They ran impressive workshops for patients on a wide variety of topics and I asked "What do you do about grief?" The question led to more questions and to me getting on my soapbox about how important it is to address grief/loss and the need for direct attention to this kind of trauma. This led to writing a proposal and starting my first workshop.

I did sweat, as I sat in that room with eight anxious faces, nine including my own. My instinctive knowing kicked in as eight pairs of eyes, curious and hesitantly looked at me and I began. There was a wide variety of loss in the room. Some lost parents, children, dear friends, unconditional loving pets. There were losses from suicide, overdoses, tragic accidents and cancer. I began the process and patients leaned in; they could see themselves in their sharing and fears began to be shed. There is nothing like that feeling of knowing you have helped someone to not feel alone, made sense of their experience or helped them shed the heaviness and guilt, or assisted in guiding them toward peace with the bits and pieces that they have been wrestling with, sometimes for years.

The more workshops I do, the more energy I have, the more I know I am on the right track and living my purpose. Patients often ask, "How do you do this? How can you hear these stories of tragedy, sadness, pain, and longing, and do it again and again?" The answer is I feel I get as much as I give. I found a way to walk that line between being emotionally overwhelmed and paralyzed by others' tragedy and loss or being callused and uncaring. This allows me to continue the work, my passion and my mission.

So here we go! There are five writing assignments for you. They can be done in a week if you are an overachiever, or over two months depending on your readiness, your ease with writing and the amount of emotion around each WE. Are you ready to write and if not, what holds you back? You might need to spend time with this question and honor any resistance you may feel (it's part of the process, too). Try to find a balance where you feel you are actively involved, but not pushing yourself too hard or too fast. You need time to write, but you also need time to process, contemplate and feel about what you are writing.

Each WE is a piece of the puzzle moving you, connecting you to your feelings and helping you notice where you may be stuck. The 5 WE's help you remember, honor and let go as you sift through your relationship with your loved one and the life journey you shared. If you work with a therapist, you may want to discuss this project with them and share and process your writings under their kind listening ear.

Those who like homework, or connect with writing, and journaling may find this process particularly helpful. I've had great success with this method; clients seem to resonate with the 5WE's and after one loss has been grieved, use the process again to bring forth healing from other unresolved losses. Over the years I've collected comments from clients, and here are a few I've often heard about the 5WE's:

- *The writing process was extremely helpful.*

- *It helped to put thoughts and feelings into words.*

- *I found purpose, learning and enlightenment.*

- *It was an excellent roadmap.*

- *It allowed me to lean into my grief and express my feelings.*

- *I was able to look at my mixed feelings about my loss and honor them all.*

- *This was a tough subject, but Gigi took us from a dark place to smiles.*

Each time I share the 5WE's; I'm grateful for the power it has to open the door to healing. Participants use words like "peace," "freedom," "acceptance," and "understanding" to describe the shifts in their feelings after completion of this work. They let go, or at least open the door to letting go, of guilt, shame, heavy feelings, and self-destructive behaviors they may have been harboring.

I've shared this method with hundreds of clients and patients through individual work and in intensive workshops. I must say, doing this work feeds my soul and pushed me to write this book. When I began working with my book coaches, they had lots of questions about what I wanted to share and my goals in writing this book. Without their curiosity, and interest I'd still be on page three! When I explain the 5WE's, my passion ignites and seems to catch on with others. My friends Gina and Natalie asked "Are you sure you want to just give this away?" My answer was an immediate "Yes! I have to. I am compelled to reach, touch, and help as many people as I possibly can!" I can continue personal work in my private practice and workshops, but I cannot reach all those who are suffering with grief. And here we are!

The Five Written Expressions of Grief™ is a creative process. I laid out a roadmap for you to follow, but within the process, there is room for free thinking to make this process your own. Sometimes healing occurs when you step outside the box. Don't get stuck on the idea of doing it right, or anticipating how long each writing should be, or what style you write it in. That will interfere with you being IN the process. You may write poetry or prose. You may write an Expression as a letter to your loved one; a logical factual minded person may write in bullet points or another favorite format that you are accustomed to. There's no limit to the ways in which you express yourself. Go for it! Knowing yourself is key. Asking yourself "How do I best work through challenges in my life?" is a good start. If you're a "color within the lines" type, what follows will flow nicely for you as you follow the directions. If you're a fan of structure and direction, here you go.

Trust yourself as you move through the process. Patients too often will start sharing by justifying the way they wrote, or saying "I'm not sure I did it right," even after all my assurances. I cannot stress enough that there is no right or wrong way to do the writings. There are ways to individualize this process that I've not seen or thought of yet. As I tell my clients and patients, however you choose to do it...it will be perfect! I mean that!

You do you!

Okay, now that I have hopefully hooked you on the project, there is some preliminary work to be done. Prior to beginning the 5 WE's there are two assignments to complete. Assignment number one: find an empty book or journal. This journal should be one that speaks to you and speaks of the person you have lost. Perhaps the journal is their favorite color, has a saying on the cover that they loved, or a picture of an activity, like sailing, golf, or gardening that was important to them. A serious looking book might fit a serious personality. One client who wrote about his Father bought a brown leather-bound journal to match his Father's serious nature and long career in law. But maybe a whimsical and playful journal would be more fitting in your case.

I've seen beautiful journals hand decorated with words, pictures and bling to bring alive the character of a cherished loved one. Don't settle, take your time to find the book. This is an important step in the process. You will know the right book when you see it! It may leap out at you or you might even have a journal at home waiting for this purpose.

The next step before beginning the writings is to select a picture of your loved one. Choose a picture that's a window to who they were. You might say "Typical Sam, doing what he loved best" or "Look at Tina with that big grin on her face." Pictures carry memories and emotions. Going through photo albums old school style or through digital files in your computer or phone, you may rediscover experiences you shared, trips and events. That smile now missing from your life, may be looking right at you, sweeping your heart away once again. Notice how you feel as you go through these memories, and take the time to capture the joy that connected you to this person in life.

Again, take your time with this. It's as important as anything else you will do moving forward. You may choose more than one picture, perhaps one of the person alone and another of your loved one with you or family and friends, representing a fond memory or adventure. One Mother mourning the loss of her son, had so many wonderful pictures of this beautiful boy as he grew up. Her son would get interested in a new toy, sport or superhero every few months. She had a hard time picking pictures so she made her journal a scrapbook with pictures fitting each of her writings. It was awesome! Once you have the picture or pictures, tape them in the front cover of your journal. It will inspire the writing to come. This book now belongs to the memory of your loved one.

Now you are ready to begin *The Five Written Expressions of Grief* ™

CHAPTER 9

The First Written Expression

REMEMBRANCE

Now it's time to write the First Written Expression, Remembrance. I call this "Write me a picture." Write a full description of your loved one. Describe them fully, from appearance to quirks and mannerisms. How did they dress? Stand? Laugh? What was important to them? What did they stand for or were willing to duke it out over? Describe them mentally and emotionally. Were they happy and easy-going? Intense, depressed, moody and worried about every little thing? What was their path in life? Who were they in relation to you? A mentor? Your rock? What was the saying they used to use when you felt down or indecisive? Were they the person you tried so hard to please and win over? Did they have years of life before you met them? What were they like when they were younger? What made them special to you and to the world? To their family and friends?

This description should be so vivid that if you read it to someone who did not know your loved one and that person later entered a room with 20 people that met the general physical description of your loved one, they could easily locate your loved one. They might recognize the loved one's interaction with others, or their look, dress, or laugh.

I start the journaling with this description because clients have voiced the fear that they will forget. They might not recall their lost love's smile, laugh, tone of their voice, or special qualities that made them a gift in their lives and others. The longer the amount of time since the loss, the more likely you are to recall less clearly. This first expression is meant to capture that.

Please remember, this should be an accurate picture of your loved one. It should include good and not so good characteristics, behaviors and experiences. It may be surprising how much you have to say. As you continue to write more, a vivid picture of them emerges. Stories and memories you have not thought of in years may come to mind. Capture them in these pages. In my workshops, sharing by another participant often triggers a memory or other information to be added to the description of your own loved one.

If you have memory gaps or were young when the loss occurred, this is a time to ask for help. Call a family member, close friend or others who knew the person well. Ask questions about their childhood years, their teens and young adult years. Who were they before you arrived in their lives? What kind of co-worker, parent, business owner and friend were they?

When Jason wrote about his Mother, he had little memory of her as she died when he was 11. When I met him, he was 52.

He had carried a sense of loss all these years. His Father was still living as was his Mother's Sister, so he made a series of calls and visited them and enjoyed unraveling the mystery of his Mother's life and history. He felt he knew her much better after his writing was complete.

When satisfied with your writing, let it rest. You may return to it several times as thoughts and memories inspire you to write more. There is no right or wrong way to do this process. You may feel you have described your loved one and their life in one page or eight pages and you may still feel there is more to say. When it feels complete, leave room for additional stories and memories, perhaps five to ten pages.

"He is in your heart,
mind and soul,
every day,
every minute"

~ GV

Remembrance

My Mother, Verna, was one of five children, being the youngest she was spoiled and as she got older was used to getting what she wanted. Verna was tall and thin. She had short brown hair but liked to color it with swatches of blue or purple. She carried herself like she was walking on air. She loved nice clothes and was a shopper always excited about a big sale and how much she saved versus spent. She liked bright colors and had her own quirky style.

She loved to cook and made elaborate Sunday meals when I was growing up. I adored my Mom and would snuggle up to her in the evenings to watch a show. She always made time for me and my brother, attending all our school activities, sports and plays. She gave honest assessments of how I performed, sometimes painful to hear, but I could trust her. I felt safe when she was around. She was an accountant in the same office for over twenty years and took care of the finances at home.

She liked plays, vanilla ice cream, the sound of thunderstorms, planting her garden, and of course getting a good deal. She had lots of friends and was relied upon for advice - for me as well. Mom put on a brave face when she got sick, but I could see the pain in her eyes. Even so, she would try to focus our time together on what I was doing and how the grandkids were. I miss her so much and that will never stop...

CHAPTER   10

The Second Written Expression

THE G.R.R.S.

Guilts, Regrets, Resentments and Sorry's,
or as I call them, the GRRS's.

(Pronounced as gerr, like a growl).

This is an often-dreaded topic, but likely to be the one keeping you stuck or longing for relief when it comes to your grief. I can almost hear the heavy sigh as you read these words. I know, this is a tough Expression to write and face for some of us. This is where you may have spent, and continue to spend, a lot of time over-thinking, analyzing, and bargaining with yourself and loved ones.

There are other feelings that can cause you to decompensate and become stuck in your grief but guilt is like hitting a wall full force in your grieving process. There is no forward movement. This guilt may be directed toward self and the things you wish you would have done or not done, said or not said. You may beat yourself over the head with all these "possible" alternative endings to the story. You may try to rewrite the story of your loved one with an ending that is happier, more connected.

As for resentment, it may be directed toward the person that is gone, their life circumstances, the rules of the road, the medical community, our source of faith, past events that caused hurt... it's an endless list. Resentments may have been building over long periods of time, grudges held, arguments unsettled, behaviors that we just cannot seem to let go of or settle. Contact with the person may have been limited because of these resentments.

We second-guess the things we said, the actions we didn't take, and try to negotiate a different outcome. We have "magical thinking" that we alone could have changed the state of our relationship before the loss or the circumstances that took our loved one away. We beat ourselves up with GRRS's and experience sleeplessness nights and unproductive days. We may have tried to stuff or bury these thoughts and feelings, but they rear their ugly heads anyway, despite our best efforts. This is the heaviness you may be holding in your body, causing headaches, stomach upset, or a heavy heart.

For some of you, these words may come easily as the subject has been on your mind so much that you cannot focus on life responsibilities in front of you. The GRRS's are often the reasons you feel unresolved in your grief. This is the time to pour out all you have been harboring in your mind and heart. Imagine your mind as a container full of thoughts swirling around like jumping beans. Now imagine removing the container, dumping all those thoughts and feelings onto the paper, and shaking out the container until it is empty...clutter and worry free. This can be a freeing, cathartic experience.

Some of us find that we have few GRRS's to report. If your relationship was uncomplicated and was full of more happy memories and lessons than worrisome events and tough love conversations, this second expression may be brief. You may have more "sorrys," as "sorrys" relate to more general sadness around loss, and find there are few regrets and guilts to emote.

Putting these thoughts on paper acknowledges thoughts and feelings that may have been living only in your subconscious mind. It frees us to be honest with ourselves about what we are experiencing. Once it has shaken loose and taken form on paper, you may find after reviewing it, that you have no further need to continue to think or react to the GRRS because they have lost the intensity and weight they had in the past. You might now see unrealistic fears or wishful thinking as feelings that only someone with super powers could have changed. It leads to thoughts of "Now that I see it on paper or say it out loud, it either makes sense or I am being unrealistic."

So, put it all out there: the things you did or didn't do, and words you said or wish you had spoken. Don't forget things your loved one did or did not do. What do you feel guilty about? What regrets do you have about this person's life, your relationship or the way the person's life played out? What are you sorry for? There may be some regrets related to particular incidents, and situations. There may also be general "sorry's" about the empty space they have left in your life and what they will miss being a part of. Perhaps there are "sorrys" about what they experienced or their pain or suffering.

This is your chance to give voice to, and let go of, thoughts and situations you have been carrying or ruminating over, and the bargaining (I wish, what if) that tied you into the pain of grief. GRRS can suck the energy out of you and create some of the heaviness we discussed earlier.

This is a challenging Expression to write. There may be a wide range of emotions. Allow them to come. Remember the way to healing is through the feelings. As we say in therapy, it may feel overwhelming or even more painful before you get relief. Pay attention and notice if these sorrows and guilts belong to you. Have you taken responsibility for your loved one's actions, decisions or tragic ending? This may be the time where you have "ah-ha's" about your role, co-dependent behaviors, your boundaries or lack thereof. Pay attention to the shifts in your feelings and thoughts.

My hope is that when you finish processing these thoughts and feelings and come out the other side, you may feel lighter. Do not get confused by thinking holding on tight to the pain of grief is a way to hold on to the person. I have seen this frequently. It is a misunderstanding that if we love and we lose love, it must be painful and that the amount of pain reflects the importance of, and caring we had, for the person. When our pain diminishes, we are not being unfaithful to our loved one. To the contrary, it is love and connection that solidifies a person's loving place in your heart. We don't have to feel tortured to keep their memory alive or prove how important they were to us. Refocus on joy.

"Regret is the aftertaste of the relationship"

~ GV

Again, when you feel this writing is complete, leave space for additional thoughts. Leave five to ten pages before moving on to the next writing.

The GRRS's

GRRS for my Brother Jim who lost his battle with alcohol and drugs at age 24:

- *I feel guilty that I didn't spend more time with you, especially as you started to struggle with alcohol and drugs, I should have been there for you.*

- *I feel guilty that I didn't push you harder to get help.*

- *I regret not saying I love you more.*

- *I regret that you wouldn't listen and slow down.*

- *I regret I haven't shared more with my kids about who you were.*

- *I regret I have not kept your memory alive.*

- *I resent drugs and that they took you away from us.*

- *I resent that you took advantage of our parents and all the pain you caused our family.*

- *I resent that you did not complete your treatment.*

- *I resent that I relapsed after you died.*

- *I am sorry you felt so defeated and alone and couldn't come to me.*

- *I am sorry you won't be here to have a family of your own.*

- *I am sorry you were in so much pain. I am sorry I did not stop to feel my own pain after you died.*

- *I am sorry you are not here.*

CHAPTER 11

The Third Written Expression

HONORING AND LOVE

This is a time to honor who this person was for you and the world. Some loved ones have had big impacts on the world; others impact their communities or were steady securing leaders within the family. How do you want to honor their lives and legacy?

Over the years I have seen so many wonderful and creative ways to honor the life of a loved one. We may honor them by finishing a task, goal, or dream they had; practicing lessons you learned from them; or setting up a fund to help others struggling with the same disease. Be creative. This may come easily and you may find a clear direction, or it may require some time and thought. You don't have to travel to foreign lands or build monuments. It might be as simple as carrying on the tradition of family dinners, or sharing stories to keep their memory alive with the next generation. Do what feels right.

Honoring can go a long way toward healing. As I am typing this, I know that I'm honoring my Father and my friend Monica. They would each be proud to know that I have kept my promise to write this book to help others struggling with grief. If my prideful Father were still here, he might act as he did in the past and take most of the credit!

Consider these questions to help you to write about lost loved ones: What did you admire about them? What made you proud? What were their gifts and strengths? How did they face challenges in their lives? What did they stand for and fight for? Honoring those we lost celebrates them and their lives. It keeps them close to our hearts and minds. They lived and left an indelible imprint on you and others.

Writing to honor their life and legacy may be easy for you. Or you may have to challenge yourself and be creative. I have been delighted to learn how clients have chosen to honor their loved ones. One young man whose Mother was a teacher for over 40 years decided to do volunteer work in the schools. Another client honored her Father by building a park full of trees in his cherished neighborhood. Others chose to honor by ending their own suffering, and remaining sober, returning to school, or fulfilling a dream of their own, to celebrate the impact of a loved one.

These actions guide you further down the road toward healing. I believe people want to DO something, do anything. Loss can make you feel helpless and this Written Expression can provide a sense of purpose.

Once you have written about honoring, it's time to turn your attention to the love you had for and with your loved one. This is the time to write about what you loved about them. Share your love for them, the love they gave to others and the way they lived their lives in these next pages. Maybe it's their character, their stubbornness, integrity, work ethic, the time they spent with you even when they had other pressures, and how they contributed to the happiness in your life or influenced the person you are today.

Some of us have had tumultuous relationships with our loved ones and may find this writing difficult. I have found we can usually come up with something positive and lovable about even a troubled loved one or a troubled relationship.

This writing may be joyful and fill you with good memories. It may lead you back to your first writing of Remembrance, to add important facts, stories and memories. Again, once you feel satisfied with your writing, leave five to ten pages. More memories and stories will show up as you work through this process. Capture them in this keepsake.

Reese wrote Honoring and Love for his Father who died after a long fight with cancer. They had a complicated relationship and were not on the best terms when he died. Reese had little contact with his Father in his young adulthood and tried to reunite when he started his own family. He felt he was making all the effort and his Father continued to disappoint him with empty promises to visit and get to know his grandchildren. Reese did not know how to feel about this loss. He knew there was a gap, a place within himself that felt hollow and empty, yet he was also holding fast to his anger and the hurt of abandonment.

Honoring and Love

Dad,

I want to honor you by getting help for myself to heal from the emptiness I sometimes feel. When I am honest with myself, I know there was a part of me that loved you and craved the connection that fathers and sons should have. I will honor you by building and maintaining that bond with my own son. I will show my honor by teaching my kids how to fish, as you taught me.

As for love, to be honest, I was not sure what I would write here...I had to search my memories, but I did love you. I loved that you were there for part of my childhood. I loved the big belly laughter that would fill the room and the way your dimples would stand out, reminding me of my own. I loved that you tried to live with integrity and listened attentively when we reunited. I love that you took responsibility for your shortcomings as a Father and said the words I am sorry. I love that I know you loved me.

After Reese shared his writing, he became quiet, then emotional. He explained he was sorting out a lot of feelings that had been ignored or tucked away. He had a question for me. He said, "How did you do that? How did you help me find love for my father?" Reese found some of the pain of abandonment and the anger melted away, leaving only the sadness of a

boy missing his father. He had been carrying around
this anger and denial of the significance of this loss
for six years.

"If you write
what you love about them,
it will give you
ideas how to honor them"

~ GV

CHAPTER 12

The Fourth Written Expression
GRATITUDE

It is time to remember and write about all the things you are grateful for within the history of your relationship with your loved one. In general, we don't spend enough time living in the light of gratitude and appreciation. I frequently give my clients homework around this topic, as it seems to help when they struggle with challenges or trauma. It's a good way to start or end your day, with a mind focused on thankfulness.

This Written Expression may seem similar to the Honoring and Love you previously wrote, but there will be distinct differences. Gratitude means thankfulness and appreciation. Have you noticed that sometimes you feel grateful when you reflect on events without recognizing the feeling at the moment? How often do you skip saying the words "Thank you?"

One gift grief gives is discovering or re-discovering gratitude. We feel gratitude for many things in our lives, if we stop to be present with them. Simple things, as well as things with enormous impacts on our lives, bring gratitude. We may regret we did not stay in the moment when grateful feelings came, or that we were so distracted we did not say, "Thank you," or "I'm so grateful for what you did for me or brought into my life."

It's never too late to feel, show, and share these experiences and words of gratitude. You may have had grateful moments that changed your life or moved you in a different direction. Gratitude may be the cornerstone that built your confidence or reminded you that you are important or loved. Now is the time to put these words and memories on paper. When we are mirrored in the face of gratitude we thrive. Again, leave space in your pages for other memories where gratitude was prominent that come to mind later.

> *"Sometimes we can get so hooked into the fact they are gone, that we lose sight that they lived."*
>
> ~ GV

Kimberly writes to her best friend Gwen who she knew since they were in middle school. Gwen lost her battle with cancer just 18 months ago at age 29.

Gratitude

Gwen,

I am so grateful that I had you in my life for so many years. I thank you for always being there for me. When Don picked on me in middle school, you stood up for me. I think that was when our friendship began. Thank you for just being your happy, optimistic self. It helped me to see the bright side of things. I so appreciate being like another sister to you, and being included in your family. Thanks for the times you listened to me, without judgement, as I worked my way through problems with family, boyfriends and later on career choices. I don't think I would have taken some of the leaps of faith I did without you being in my corner.

I am grateful for your laugh, your energy, and optimism, and your comfort with being yourself. I learned how to "do me" from watching you. I am also grateful that I could be with you when you received your diagnosis. I remember us crying together and then moving forward to make the best of the time you had left. Thank you for not pushing me away and allowing me to help with your care as you grew weaker. There was no place else I would rather be. Even then, toward the end, you worried about how I was doing. Thank you for this and so many unselfish acts over the years. You mean the world to be, you are my bestie. :)

The person I am now will always be impacted by you and our friendship. I appreciate our special bond and hope to live up to your dreams for me.

Thank you, my friend,
Kim

CHAPTER 13

The Fifth
Written Expression
LETTING GO/HOLDING ON

The Fifth Expression is the culmination of the other writings. As you reflect on your memories, regrets, honoring, and gratitude, you may want to summarize them as they have brought you to a place where you can look at what you want and/or need to hold on to or let go of. I would never suggest that you let go of your loved one. I believe this process will help you hold tighter to them in the healthiest way.

The purpose of this process is to note situations, regrets, and negative or heavy feelings that it is time to let go of. These may have prevented you from honoring the relationship and finding the peace you are looking for. Again, I would warn against the urge to hold on to intense pain as a show of love or devotion. Continued pain is unnecessary and will only obscure the sincerity of your intentions and feelings for your loved one. There will likely be many memories you never want to forget. If they transformed your life (even though uncomfortable or challenging at the time) hold on to them. Take some time to think about what serves you well and enriches your life. Hold on to lessons that have guided you and let go of what holds you back, interferes with your happiness and connection to others or stands in the way of releasing remaining pain, heaviness or regret.

My hope is that you will feel lighter after this fifth writing. I truly believe that those we have loved, those who have gone before us, want us to embrace joy and peace. Our loved ones have no need for us to beat ourselves up over something in the past or to drown in sad or overwhelming feelings of loss.

I often ask clients, "What would your Father/Sister/Best Friend/Mentor/Partner say if they saw how you were feeling?" Most people know the answer and can even picture them delivering the lecture. They want to be remembered, and they want you to be okay and use the experience of this loss as a way to be more present and live more fully.

> *"You can move on*
> *and hold on*
> *at the same time"*
>
> ~ GV

Jason lost his Mother when he was 11 years old and carried the loss and sadness until he was almost 52. He wrote his Mom a letter. It's never too late to grieve...

Letting Go and Holding On

Mom,

It is hard for me to say goodbye. Even after all these years I don't feel ready. I don't understand why you had to leave my life when I was so young. I struggle with losing you. Please help me to understand that you are alright and that we are still together in spirit.

I can imagine so many things we could have done together if we had more time, yet I am grateful for the time we did have. Please help me to remember all the time we had together, the good memories, and the lessons you taught me. I thank you for all the love you showed me and all that you did for me.

Still, there are so many experiences and events I wish I could have shared with you. I have come to believe that you have always been here with me, watching over me. Remind me of your presence, especially when I need your comfort and support. Guide me so I can be the person I want to be for myself and my family. Help me be the person you'd be proud of.

Mom, I will always miss you. I love you. I believe we have an unbreakable bond and are connected. If there is anything you ever need, I will be right here.

My Love Always,
Your Devoted Son,
Jason

Letting Go + Holding On

Caroline was in her late forties when we met. She came to see me about her struggle with her body image and continual weight gain that had frustrated her over the last few years. Caroline had been committed to her six-year-old son Damen. They spent hours playing games, reading, and exploring the world. One day Damen sneaked outside, wanting to pick flowers for his Mother, and tripped and fell into the pool. Caroline lived with guilt and despair that played out in her life for more than twenty years.

She chose relationships where she was treated poorly, feeling she did not deserve anything more. She turned to alcohol as a way of disappearing, numbing the pain of her loss. And finally, she tried to fill this emptiness with food. When I asked "the magic question" this story unfolded. I believe all her years of self-destructive behavior stemmed from the loss of her son.

Letting Go

There are so many things to let go of. You, my beautiful son, are not one of them. I will hold you close to my heart and continue to think of you for as long as I breathe. I will, however, bid farewell and let go of some things that held me back from honoring you, and living fully.

I let go of the guilt and blaming myself.

I say goodbye to the bargaining and "what if's" that run through my head.

I let go of crying and holding onto heavy emotions, so I can make room to hold on to laughter, joy and loving relationships I have pushed away but now I have the belief that I deserve,

I say farewell to the numbness, running from my pain, feeling alone, and filling my sense of emptiness with food.

I reject all the negative thoughts, and deeds that stand in the way of the pure love I will always have for you.

I say farewell to the past and welcome a happy and hopeful future.

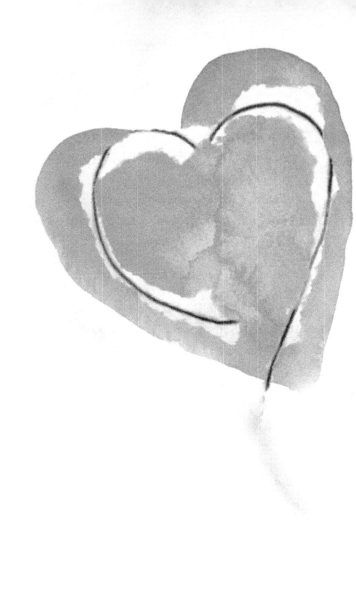

SECTION THREE

The Longer Journey Toward Healing

This last section is a resource for you as you continue your journey toward healing. I include commonly asked questions, and offer professional advice and support. I hope you find reassurance in these words that your experiences are normal, and you feel accepted as you continue your journey. This section may be a resource and reference when you are struggling with grief and new questions. As time goes on, you may be prompted to review this advice, it is there for you, whenever the need arises.

The Light

I was lost.

Wondering in a mist of pain,

heart pounding,
signaling my awareness,
my knowing,

that something had shifted
without you,

without your
touch,
laugh,
proximity.

Yet, the clouds broke,

showing light beyond the mist,

bringing gifts of hope that
showered my despair.

Holding you tight in my
mind and heart,

memories, laughter, connection,

blanketing me with comfort,

nourishing my soul and

illuminating the
gifts you've left me.

BY GIGI VEASEY

CHAPTER 14

The Questions You Want to Ask

"I've Gotta Question For Ya"

When I lost my dear friend Monica tragically, I became even closer to her Husband, LJ. We were friends before and enjoyed our outings and gatherings. But after this tragedy, we became much closer and would talk almost daily during those first three months. We would share our thoughts, feelings and the dreams we had. We talked about how things had changed in our lives without Monica. After a while, knowing I was a psychotherapist and grief and loss was my specialty, LJ asked for my thoughts, feelings, and opinions about what he was experiencing. Most of those conversations started with: "I've gotta question for ya." I knew this was a time for me to listen, learn, and to share my knowledge, personally and professionally.

So many questions arise after a loss. Some questions people don't know how to ask, or even if it's okay to ask. We may not trust ourselves to make decisions or handle various situations that arise. Inability to identify feelings can further lead to the list of unasked and unanswered questions. We may question the way we think. We may wonder "When can I finally talk about these burning questions?" Some questions I hear frequently are: "Is it okay for me to have fun? To laugh?" "How long will this painful loneliness go on?" "Do I have to keep talking about what happened to my loved one?" "Do I have to get rid of their belongings?" "Is it okay to feel some relief?" "Can I be angry with God, The Universe, or my Higher Power?" "When would it be okay to date or connect with someone new?" As we move through grief, there are many avenues of life to ponder and adjustments to make in the space left behind.

These questions may arouse shame or create fear that others will not understand or find such questions heartless, unloving, or unfaithful to the lost loved one. That is not the case. There are rarely wrong or inappropriate questions, but there are often unasked questions. Questioning is natural, and I think it is a necessary part of grief. If you've never really grieved before, navigating the challenges, changes in routine, and emptiness, may come with much hesitation and many questions. The list above is not an inclusive list of questions keeping people up at night after a loss, but it's a start. Let's begin to navigate some answers and options to help on your continued journey toward healing.

Do I have to keep talking about what happened?

It helps and soothes some people to share openly about their loss, though some might not have a trusted confidant to hear their pain. Just telling your story can be healing. Sharing can create a sense of not being alone. Knowing yourself and what is helpful or not helpful for YOU is key. Some don't want to continually talk about their loss because it brings up painful feelings. To get through day-to-day life, we may distance ourselves from the pain of loss, and feelings of guilt, regret, or sadness. We don't want to "feel" all the time. It can be exhausting! Let people know what you need, what helps you and what doesn't.

It's okay to be direct. It's okay to say "I am really not comfortable talking about this" or "When I talk about my loss, it just brings up painful feelings for me." There is no single "right" way. Do what feels best for you. Advocate for yourself, keeping what's best for you in mind.

How long will I feel this way?

Everybody is different. Some people move through the intensity of grief in a healthy way in short periods of time, and feel genuinely at peace with it. Others struggle for years. I spoke with someone earlier today, and asked, "How often do you think about your Mom?" He responded "I think about my Mom every single day." There is a strong possibility he remains in deep grieving or is stuck somewhere in the process. Avoid judging yourself. Be kind to yourself on this continual journey. Grieving is far from a logical or set in concrete experience. Don't let your mind over-shadowing your heart.

If I don't cry, does it mean I am not grieving?

No, it does not mean you are not grieving. Everyone's experience is unique when grieving and expressing emotions. Sometimes crying seems the obvious or appropriate reaction to a loss. Reflecting on other times in your life when you experienced loss or sorrow may give you a glimpse of how you're likely to react while grieving. Some of us realize we are not big criers. You can express grief in the ways that fit for you and the situation of loss that you are experiencing. You can feel sadness, sorrow, and pain without crying. There may be other outward symbols of your sorrow. Don't compare yourself to others or hold unreasonable expectations.

I feel tired all the time, and I can't focus. Is that normal?

Grievers have often not heard that grief is not just an emotional state. It is also visceral, affecting us physically. Physical fatigue accompanies grieving. You may feel heavy and restless. This may not be recognized as fatigue related to grief. You may think you are coming down with something. I often agree "Yes, you are coming down with something. You are coming down with grief." Self-care is important as you grieve and heal. Use your support system and leave room for naps and rest.

Is it okay to feel relieved that my loved one is not suffering anymore?

This question often comes with loss after significant suffering. If your loved one has suffered through a long illness or sudden intense illness, there is bound to be some relief that they are no longer struggling. I think people have some hesitation about feeling relief. The relief brings up feelings of guilt. If you think about relief, it is about the end of their painful journey. I see grievers tether guilt to their feelings of relief. "If I feel relieved, I have to feel guilty that I feel relieved."

Shame around feelings of relief may closely follow. You are in good company. When there is suffering, from physical, mental/emotional illness or addiction, thoughts of and hopes for relief from the struggle and pain your loved one lives with are common. It is okay to feel relief. It is a normal natural part of grieving. It is not a selfish expression of grief. The relief may be for them, yourself and/or other loved ones. It can be a loving expression of grief and loss. I encourage this reframing.

Many people suffered for long periods of time. The kindest thing we can do is wish for release from that pain, and for them to have peace.

I am a perfectionist. What if I am grieving wrong?

There is no wrong way to grieve, with this caveat; as long as you are engaged with your feelings. As I have said before, "The healing is through the feelings." We each grieve differently. There is a broad range of grieving in a healthy way. Avoid comparing yourself to others when you are grieving. There is no perfect way to grieve. Anytime we are striving for perfection, we are likely to be disappointed and feel we have fallen short. Strive not for perfection, but to be you. Grieve in the healthiest way for you! Remember, there is no right way as long as you are feeling those feelings.

Why do I feel bad when I take care of myself?

Don't get self-care confused with being selfish, especially when grieving. It is not selfish to take care of yourself. It's being 'self-full' which is a healthy practice. You have to take care of yourself before you can take care of anyone else. When grieving, managing our self-care is even more important. Our bodies, mentally, physically, emotionally and spiritually, need extra attention at that time. We do it for ourselves and we do it for all the other people around us.

I feel better when I keep busy. Is that healthy?

Distraction is sometimes helpful for grief; it can provide temporary relief. It is hard to be in the throes of grief all the time. Distraction helps us feel closer to normal, and feel a little bit more in control. Staying occupied and being productive can create a sense of control and a sense of purpose. Both can be helpful when grieving. We can become overwhelmed if we don't distract ourselves sometimes. If distraction becomes your primary mode of functioning, take a closer look and make time to be present with your loss and feelings.

Am I running from my grief?

Thinking that you are not feeling enough or are not grieving "properly" may have you wondering if you are running from your grief. That can make you ask if you are saddened or emotional enough, or thinking of them enough. We want to grieve right, but there is really no right way as long as you are experiencing your feelings, you are in process. We can get side tracked while grieving by self-made or circumstantial distractions. We may turn to the use of substances to numb, or become so busy we don't stop to think and feel. We can disappear emotionally and give our loss little thought.

Keeping busy with activities, work, or projects leaves little time to ponder what you are experiencing. This may come from fear of "If I really began to feel about this, I might become overwhelmed." Checking in with yourself and asking "Am I being present with my feelings?" can be helpful. A sense of being overwhelmed is not needed to indicate you are experiencing grief. Some of our feelings come up in a gentler way and this is okay.

Is it alright for me to be angry with God, the Universe, or with my Higher Power?

Anger can be a necessary and important part of grieving. Yes, it is alright to be angry with God, the Universe, your Higher Power or whatever spiritual foundation guides your life. Whatever you believe, that faith can handle the burden of your anger while you heal. It is essential to allow yourself to have all your feelings, even the uncomfortable ones. Express your anger in a healthy way, knowing that it is not likely to last forever. Yes, tragedy can shake your beliefs and this re-evaluation may take some time. You may find your way back to beliefs that guided your life, or a new foundation of belief may emerge.

Is it acceptable that my partner and I experience grief differently?

Yes! It is unlikely that two people will experience grief in the same way, especially the loss of a child. Each parent will grieve differently. Questions arise: "What happened?" "Was it sudden, random, or anticipated?" "Is there a sense of guilt, or blame, or responsibility for the loss?" These questions affect the way you grieve. Two people will have two different experiences and insights. The relationship with the loved one was unique to each partner. We are 'emotionally individual,' sharing and showing our emotions in individual expression.

Some of us are outwardly in our grief, want to talk, and have lots of questions. Others have the impulse to do something, take some action, or find some kind of purpose. Still others are quiet about their grief.

You and your partner will experience different emotions at different times, and different triggers, even though you had the same love for the one you lost. Don't judge the way your partner grieves. If you are in sync with your feelings, moods and healing process, this is an extra blessing.

Is it okay to be angry with my loved one?

Yes. Anger is an important and often necessary part of grieving. We can be angry at so many things, including our loved one. We may be angry because they decided they no longer wanted treatment or "gave up the fight." We may be angry because we have so much pain, miss them greatly or feel alone. We can be angry because of some of their decisions and actions. Anger may show up simply because they are not here anymore. There are lots of reasons to be angry and it's okay to be angry with them. Anger often harbors fear and hurt. It can be helpful to reflect on these underlying feelings. They can lead you closer to peace.

If I don't stay in pain, will I forget them?

A big myth about grief and love is that my display of pain shows how much I love someone, and the intensity of my love is mirrored by the intensity of my pain. Some grievers have a stranglehold on their pain, or wear it like a symbol of love. You do not need it. Focus on the good feelings and memories that honor the people that you love. Lean in to them. I understand the fear of forgetting. You can use the Five Written Expressions to hold those memories and create a keepsake. Pain does not have to be the way you hold on. It is okay to let go of the intensity of the pain.

Grief illuminates those thoughts, more than at other times in life. When we have a loss, we self-reflect on who we are, where we are, what we are doing, how we spend our time, who we love, what's important, and what's not. All of these questions arise when we grieve. If these thoughts become intense or intrusive, for long periods of time, then you may want to seek some advice. I believe this is one of the gifts of grief. Grief can be a mirror exposing deeper thoughts, leading us to finding and embracing more meaning, purpose, and connection in our lives.

If it's been years since my loss. Why do I still feel so sad?

If it has been years since you lost your loved one and sadness continues to feel intense, it may indicate it's time to get some help. Intense sadness might be triggered by more recent losses reminding us of the pain of past losses. Depressive episodes can also keep us deep in sadness longer than we may expect. Lingering sadness has many factors, such as living in a home surrounded by belongings, memories, good and bad, reminding you of your loved one.

Many things can trigger your sadness. Being aware and accepting the feeling may help you fully experience it and lead to a release of some of the intensity. Good support and seeking professional help will lead to some thoughtful questions and can help you learn what keeps you in this space and what this sadness means or symbolizes for you. Once you have some deeper understanding, it may be easier to move forward.

When will life return to normal?

"Normal" is an interesting word. I don't believe that after a loss, life is ever going to be like it was before. It's a matter of finding a new normal. Some things in life will return to routine, like going to bed, getting up, going to work, taking the kids to school, or participating in spiritual practices and other grounding activities. Some of these activities will help us feel back to normal. However, our losses, especially deep losses, will change what is normal for us indefinitely.

Is it appropriate for me to have fun, to laugh?

Yes, it is okay. Grief does not have to be exclusively a burdening, painful experience lacking room for any uplifting emotion. It does not require an overwhelming demonstration that you are grieving or how much you cared for your loved one. Most people know when they feel ready to laugh, because they simply feel like laughing. The real question is "When will my family and friends feel it is okay for me to start living again?"

We want to be respectful about our loss, but there is a difference between giving yourself time to feel and heal, and depriving yourself of joy. These two things can live within the same space. We are still here! We are here to live and it honors those that are gone when we live fully. I don't mean to say start partying on week two, but trust your gut, your intuition and the voice of your loved one in your head saying, "It's time, I want you to live, be present, and enjoy life." Tune in, the answers are there.

How long will this pain last?

The pain of loss is very personal. The intensity of that pain depends on the circumstances of the loss. Was it sudden or tragic? Was the relationship close? Strong? Complicated? We must consider our own capacity and ability to be present with all the feelings arising from loss. Stuffing those thoughts and feelings, prolongs the pain and grieving. We may feel less emotional pain initially, as numbness or shock take the lead.

If we feel a sense of responsibility; projected, imagined or real; or have other unfinished businesslike unresolved conflicts or discord, these can contribute to the pain. There are countless factors in our journey through the pain of loss. Sharing and expressing what is going on in your mind and heart can help lessen the heaviness you carry. Having open, trusting support is one avenue to ease the pain.

When can I begin to date or connect with someone new in my life?

You have to trust yourself to know when it is right. When you trust your heart and trust your gut, you will know if your motive is pure. If your motive is running from your grief or avoiding feelings, this is probably not the right time. If the decision is based on feeling you are healing, and not escaping from loneliness, your timing is probably spot on.

Judgment by others regarding your desire to move on and have a new partner can play a role in your hesitance. You may be surprised by the support and understanding you receive when you open up to those close to you about how you are feeling and possibilities for your future. Some of us move on to new relationships quickly, as we only know life as a partnership and feel lost without one. Some of us take years to move on, or choose to live solo, not imagining it any other way. Don't judge yourself harshly as you negotiate your new lifestyle.

Do I have to let go of my loved one's belongings?

Some grievers feel pressured to let go of their loved one's possessions. We often instinctively know when we are ready to let go of belongings. Desire and attachment may be strong while deep in grief, a sign it is not yet time to let go. People pressure themselves about this, feeling like it needs to happen in order for them to "move on." Honor your own time table. But if it's been years and you are still holding on to belongings, it's probably time to get help to learn why you are feeling it is so important to hold on.

Keeping some special, important items to remind you of the person you've lost, remind you of good and happy memories, or challenging times you got through together, is natural and can be important to healing. You don't have to throw out everything. Avoid the urge to be black and white about this decision. Consider going through possessions to understand what you are emotionally attached to, and how it might serve you in your grief, honoring and loving that person. Start by letting go of the things that don't have meaning to you. Trust yourself.

How will I get through this without you?

A very difficult question, especially when your loved one was the one you turned to in a crisis or they were "your person." When you are sad, overwhelmed, and hurting, and that person is no longer present, there can be a sense of emptiness no one else can fill. Continue to embrace their life, think of them, talk of them, and celebrate them. Ask them those questions: "What would my Nana do?" Or "What would my dad say, if he were here?" Asking "How would she/he support me?" can help move you toward your healing while keeping them close and honored.

When is it time to seek help with my grief?

The first year of a loss can be horrific, incredibly painful, and overwhelming. The second year may still be pretty tough, but if you get into your third year and you are still really struggling with grief, and your emotions, or lack thereof, it is time to seek help. You may be stuck somewhere in your healing. You may have had unavoidable distractions, or even sought distractions, to keep you from moving forward and healing. It's time to take a closer look as unresolved grief can reduce your ability to live fully. Reaching for outside help can also be supporting earlier in your grief, to help you to feel more calm, to be heard, understand you are not alone, and to know what to expect from this journey toward healing.

Easing the Pain & Finding Happiness & Joy Again

CHAPTER 15

Takeaways

Here are a few things I hope you will remember from our book journey as you continue to deal with your grief.

☐ *Loss is a part of life. When we face it with love and kindness toward ourselves and others, we can find a way back to living with joy.*

☐ *The healing is through the feelings. You cannot heal without going through the process.*

☐ *Grieving is not a competition.*

☐ *Most often, there are gifts in grief. Look for what was left behind for you by your loved ones.*

☐ *If you delay or avoid grieving, it will wait for you... indefinitely.*

☐ *Avoid self-criticism putting you on an imagined timeline to "move on". The goal is living on, not moving on.*

☐ *Use your support system. Don't be afraid to ask for support, advice or a kind ear when you need it.*

☐ *Writing can be very therapeutic.*

☐ *You are not alone. At any given time, someone you know is traversing the road through grief.*

☐ *Live fully, be present, seek happiness.*

☐ *Watch for the Unexplainable. These experiences can provide hope and a sense of peace.*

☐ *Speak up, stand up, allow others to support and help you.*

☐ *Trust your gut and intuition while making decisions.*

☐ *No one can ever take your memories, they live on.*

Actions You Can Take

Here are some actions to support you while grieving and keep you moving toward healing.

☐ *Continue to journal your thoughts and feelings.*

☐ *Seek medication support from your PCP or Psychiatry.*

☐ *Don't hesitate, use your support system.*

☐ *Decrease alcohol consumption.*

☐ *Manage your physical health (i.e., blood pressure, chronic pain, migraines).*

☐ *Exercise. It increases the good chemicals in your brain.*

☐ *Seek counseling, individual, family and or couples.*

☐ *Prioritize your self-care.*

☐ *Lead by example, show your feelings, speak your truth.*

☐ *Balance life, make room and time for what's important.*

☐ *Avoid isolation. Don't worry about burdening others.*

☐ *Sleep! We function better, physically and emotionally, with rest.*

☐ *Ask for help, from friends, family, and professionals.*

☐ *Set boundaries. Protect your precious time and energy.*

☐ *Practice saying "No." It's not a dirty word.*

☐ *Pray, meditate.*

☐ *Stay connected!*

☐ *Bereavement groups are available through Hospice, hospitals, and community services.*

☐ *Talk with clergy.*

☐ *Find your new normal.*

☐ *Be kind, gentle, and patient with yourself while grieving.*

☐ *Remember, it is okay to embrace life and live fully.*

☐ *Keep in mind, The Five Written Expressions of Grief, this tool is yours now, there whenever you need it.*

"*One day,
one step,
one breath
at a time*"

~ GV

E P I L O G U E

A Dream...
Wednesday, June 20th, 2018

I did what I tell my clients not to do if they have problems sleeping: doing things that activate your mind. I was working on editing and writing this book one evening until near midnight. I had a tough time sleeping and did what I call "the rotisserie." Maybe you have experienced it as well, turning from side to side, again and again, trying to find that comfortable space only to move again. As I woke up this morning to the sound of birds singing, I captured this dream....

I was living in California with my Husband and had opened a restaurant, (another dream of mine). It was opening night. I was excited and nervous. We had only drawn in five tables over the evening but I remained optimistic that it would take some time. I am sure I'm not the only one who has a rule to not go to a restaurant if there is no one in it! Go to the one with the line out the door. You can be sure the food is good.

The last table to leave was a young couple I had chatted with off and on throughout the evening. They were on vacation, a very special vacation. The young man had explained that his wife had a terminal diagnosis and this was probably their last trip to get out and explore while she was still feeling healthy. She seemed to be accepting of this, and was present and enjoying all she could on this adventure.

When they were ready to leave, the young man decided to go and get the car so his wife wouldn't have to walk. He could see the weary look on her face. I waited with her, but she suddenly became impatient and insisted on walking. I felt a little panic run through me. My Husband and I followed her as she headed down the street. As she got further away, I sent him back to lock up the restaurant. I continued to walk along, fearful about her condition and state of mind. She began to cross the street and then suddenly stopped in the crosswalk, and sat down. I ran to her and knelt down so she could feel my presence. My heart broke. A minute later her Husband drove up, scooped her up, and put her in the car. I hoped she just needed a good night's rest because she had over done it.

I pressed my card into her hand "Gigi Veasey, Psychotherapist" and handed him this book. I hoped they had more good times ahead before the inevitable and the book would give him some comfort when the time to grieve began....

I didn't set out in my career to write a book. It surprised me, but it was my passion for the subject and my need to deliver this message that drove me to it. I could not withhold the words that gave me relief in my grief or the Five Written Expressions of Grief ™ that have touched and helped so many in my practice and workshops. When I see the looks of pain and sorrow in the eyes of the clients and patients I work with, I can't help but take this resolute stance to help, to ease this pain, to share my understanding, and provide hope of not only surviving a tragic loss but holding loved ones in a special place in your heart as pain washes away and you begin finding happiness and joy in life again. After all, isn't that what your loved one would want for you?

Fine'

B I B L I O G R A P H Y

Chapter 1: Grief 101

1) Satir, Virginia. *The Satir Model: Family Therapy and Beyond* Paperback – January 1, 1994 Publisher Science and Behavior Books; Publication date January 1, 1994

https://www.goodreads.com/author/quotes/312508.Virginia Satir

2) Kubler-Ross, Elizabeth. "On Death and Dying" The 5 Stages of Grief, Published 1969. MacMillian Publishing

3) Grief: noun, Merriam-Webster Dictionary

Chapter 2: The Magic Question

4) 10%-15% of people have severe reactions to grief. "Bonanno, George A. 2004. " Loss, Trauma and Human Resilience: Have we underestimated the Human Capacity to Thrive After Extreme Aversive Events?"

5) "Broken Heart Syndrome" Reference American Heart Association, 2017, December 12 article "Is Broken Heart Syndrome real?".

6) Statistics Most of us will not reach the age of 18 without having experienced the loss of a loved one. An estimated 1 in 14, or 5.2 million, children in the U.S. will experience the death of a parent or sibling before they reach the age of 18.

Judi's House/JAG Institute partnered with the New York Life Foundation to help support grieving children and families by creating the Childhood Bereavement Estimation Model (CBEM)2020.

7) In the U.S. over 8 million people each year will suffer through the loss of an immediate family member. In the U.S., 8 million people suffered through the death of someone in their immediate family last year; 800,000 new widows and widowers; 400,000

people under 25 suffered from the death of a loved one (National Mental Health Association)

8) An estimated 800,000 people lose their spouses each year and unexpectedly become widows and widowers. Osterweis, M., Solomon, F., & Green, M. (1984). Bereavement: Reactions, consequences, and care. Washington, DC: National Academy Press.

9) Approximately 1.2 million children will not be tucked into bed by a parent who is missing from their life. 1.2 million children will lose a parent to death before age 15 *(Dr. Elizabeth Weller, Dir. Ohio State University Hospitals, 1991)*

10) There are an estimated 104 fatal car accidents each day in this country impacting families and loved ones.(NHTSA, 2009) Full cite: National Highway Traffic Safety Administration. About 115 people die every day in vehicle crashes in the United States -- one death every 13 minutes. griefspeaks.com

Chapter 3: Why Is This Important

11) Poem: "Fully Alive" by Dawna Markova

Chapter 4: What to Expect When Grieving

12) "The Old Guy" Facebook posting:

www.thatericalper.com2015/08/16

Chapter 5: When Grief Gets Messy

13) 72% of parents' relationships survive after the loss of a child. When a Child Dies: a Survey of Bereaved Parents, conducted by NFO in 1999 and published on the Web site of Compassionate Friends" (www.doorsofhope.com/grieving-healing/compassionate friends.htm).

14) Substance abuse, only 10% get help Almost 21 million Americans have at least one addiction, yet only 10% of them receive treatment.

15) Chronic Grief definition

Chapter 7: The Things You Can't Explain:

16) Toto; "Africa" The Essential Toto 1982

17) Bruce Hornsby and the Range; The Way It Is album, "Mandolin Rain" 1986

Chapter 9: The Gifts You Don't Expect:

18) Poem by Joanna Macy , no title.

About the Author

Having worked with thousands of patients across the United States, Gigi Veasey, LCSW, LISAC, CCBT, is a renowned psychotherapist and consultant in private practice in Phoenix, Arizona. Over the last 40 years, Gigi has worked in hospitals, inpatient treatment facilities, and with families and organizations helping individuals manage their experiences with grief and loss. She shares her expertise and passion through lectures, workshops, and private one-on-one sessions, and helps individuals understand that while grief and loss can create foundational changes in their lives, there is always hope for growth and healing. Gigi is also the founder of Alcohol Recovery Solutions, Inc. helping those struggling with substance use find their way through addiction, depression, anxiety, and trauma to rediscover self and move toward a hopeful, full life. Gigi lives in the beautiful desert of Phoenix, Arizona and delights in the serene mountains that surround her home and the owl family who live in her backyard.

To learn more or to schedule a private Zoom or your in-person session with Gigi, contact her at gigwoman@earthlink.net.

bigsteptorecovery.com

gigiveasey

gigi-veasey-45006a13

Notes

If you enjoyed this book

please share your opinion

with others on Amazon.com.

I would love to hear

what you have to say

and greatly appreciate

your support.

Made in the USA
Coppell, TX
15 September 2021

62421254R00138